LEADING
LIFE-CHANGING
small groups

Books in the Groups That Grow Series

Building a Life-Changing Small Group Ministry

Coaching Life-Changing Small Group Leaders

Leading Life-Changing Small Groups

Equipping Life-Changing Leaders DVD

Over 200,000 Copies Sold

Third Edition

LEADING

LIFE-CHANGING

small groups

BILL DONAHUE

 ZONDERVAN®
.com

 WILLOW
Willow Creek Resources

 GROUPS
that GROW

ZONDERVAN.com/
AUTHORTRACKER
follow your favorite authors

We want to hear from you. Please send your comments about this book to us in care of zreview@zondervan.com. Thank you.

ZONDERVAN

Leading Life-Changing Small Groups
Copyright © 2012 by Bill Donahue and Willow Creek Association

This title is also available as a Zondervan ebook. Visit www.zondervan.com/ebooks.

Requests for information should be addressed to:

Zondervan, *Grand Rapids, Michigan 49530*

Library of Congress Cataloging-in-Publication Data

Donahue, Bill, 1958–
    Leading life-changing small groups / Bill Donahue.
       p. cm.
    ISBN 978-0-310-33125-4 (softcover)
    1. Church group work. 2. Small groups—Religious aspects—Christianity. I. Title
    BV652.2.D66 2012
    253'.7—dc23
                         2011048572

Scripture quotations marked TNIV are taken from the Holy Bible, *Today's New International Version*™. *TNIV*®. Copyright © 2001, 2005 by Biblica, Inc™. Used by permission of Zondervan. All rights reserved worldwide.

All Scripture quotations marked NIV are taken from The Holy Bible, *New International Version*®, *NIV*®. Copyright © 1973, 1978, 1984 by Biblica, Inc™. Used by permission. All rights reserved worldwide.

Any Internet addresses (websites, blogs, etc.) and telephone numbers in this book are offered as a resource. They are not intended in any way to be or imply an endorsement by Zondervan, nor does Zondervan vouch for the content of these sites and numbers for the life of this book.

Cover design: Kirk DouPonce
Interior design: Sherri L. Hoffman

Printed in the United States of America

13 14 15 16 17 /DCI/ 27 26 25 24 23 22 21 20 19 18 17 16 15 14 13 12 11 10 9 8 7 6 5 4 3

Dedicated to every leader who has answered the call
to serve the kingdom of God by guiding a small group
of fellow seekers toward maturity in Christ.
May Jesus reward you for your faithfulness
and unwavering devotion to your ministry.

CONTENTS

Preface   9

Acknowledgments   13

Introduction: Becoming a Biblical Community   15

  1. Clarifying Your Purpose   25

  2. Sharpening Your Leadership   39

  3. Developing Your Apprentice   75

  4. Pursuing Spiritual Growth   87

  5. Leading Life-Changing Meetings   105

  6. Measuring Group Progress   141

  7. Caring for Members   151

  8. Impacting Your World   161

Appendix 1: Kinds of Small Groups   181

Appendix 2: Relationship-Building Exercises   182

Appendix 3: The Analytic Method of Bible Study   188

Welcome. This manual has been designed for small group leaders by small group leaders, group pastors, and ministry leaders. It is a reference guide and working document for your ministry, providing the information and resources you need to lead a transformational small group in which life change is the norm, not the exception.

HOW TO USE THIS RESOURCE

You'll find that *Leading Life-Changing Small Groups* is organized in a way that anticipates your questions, making it easy for you to find the information you need when you need it. It's also designed with a lot of common sense. Each section leads to the next. Using the tools in this book, you'll be able to lead the kind of small group that turns participants into fully devoted followers of Jesus Christ.

Throughout the material are places for you to interact, enter your own thoughts, or develop a strategy for some aspect of your ministry. Take the time to engage the material when prompted.

USING THE DVD

Complementing this resource is a DVD designed for group leaders, *Equipping Life-Changing Small Group Leaders* (sold separately; ISBN 0310331277). It will guide you through *Leading Life-Changing Small Groups* and help you understand the focus of each of the book's eight chapters. The DVD includes focused teaching, engaging dramas, and other creative elements to inspire and equip you for leadership.

Before working through each chapter, watch the corresponding DVD segment. Each video is approximately eight to ten minutes long. Once you have viewed the DVD, you can work through the material in that chapter at your own pace or with a group of leaders in your ministry. In many cases, your church leadership will be guiding the process.

HOW THE MATERIAL IS STRUCTURED

Chapter 1 begins with the underlying principles and values of biblical community, giving you a vision for group life. Beliefs give rise to actions. What you believe about community, small groups, discipleship, and leadership in the body of Christ will determine the nature of your ministry efforts. This section provides you with the core for developing a thriving and exciting ministry.

Chapter 2 strikes at the heart of a successful small group: your personal leadership. Trained, gifted, and passionate leaders form the backbone of a small group ministry intent on developing fully devoted and fruitful Christ followers. Here we address the spiritual life, responsibilities, and character of the small group leader.

Chapter 3 focuses on the successful development of additional leaders through the process of apprenticing. Shared leadership is the biblical norm; leadership is not simply the responsibility of a few paid staff members. Every group leader gets to identify, challenge, motivate, and equip people who will become future leaders of life-changing groups.

Chapter 4 teaches you how to grow the best environment for group life. After you cast a biblical vision to guide your ministry, understand your role as a leader, and commit yourself to mentoring potential leaders, you can focus on the inner workings of your group. You'll find guidance for forming your group, shaping its vision, establishing its ground rules and covenant, and understanding its communication patterns.

Chapter 5 walks you through the skills and information needed to conduct life-changing meetings—from designing a meeting to using great questions, handling conflicts, building relationships, and leading dynamic discussions. Meetings are the most catalytic aspect of your ministry, a prime opportunity to gather, build momentum, deepen relationships, and accomplish your purpose.

Chapter 6 will help you gain essential feedback to measure progress and make adjustments as you lead. Tools here will give you insights into your own leadership growth and effectiveness, as well as information about how the group is doing.

Chapter 7 has resources to help you become a shepherd and help your people become a caring group. You will learn to encourage members and create a nurturing environment where members find rest for their souls, prayer for their needs, and healing for their wounds. You will learn how to lead when a group member is in crisis or needs extreme care.

Chapter 8 lays out how to help the group impact others outside the group. You have the privilege of extending the kingdom of God beyond the group and of reaching out to others who have yet to experience the fullness of true community in Christ. You'll learn how to connect others to group life, you'll explore ways to serve others in your world, and you'll find resources for having conversations with spiritual seekers.

Finally, there are three appendixes at the back of this book: "Kinds of Small Groups," "Relationship-Building Exercises," and "The Analytic Method of Bible Study."

Dig in and get ready for the adventure of your life—leading a small group community that is producing followers of Jesus Christ, that is dedicated to one another, and that is committed to building the kingdom together.

ACKNOWLEDGMENTS

This is the third edition of *Leading Life-Changing Small Groups*, evidence that this resource has struck a chord with leaders who need practical tools for leading groups. This would not have had anywhere near the impact it has without the support, contributions, feedback, and wisdom of many others.

I am indebted to Paul Engle and the Zondervan publishing team, without whom this work would never arrive in the hands of leaders worldwide. You have broadened the scope of my ministry and introduced me to many global leaders and group life zealots. I especially want to thank John Raymond, Ryan Pazdur, Brian Phipps, and their teams for editing and guiding the work, and Mark Kemink for his marketing expertise.

Thanks also to the C2 Group and to Mike Seaton and his talented video crew, who brought my vision for the DVD material to life.

I appreciate the hard work of all those who participated in the creation of the first version of this handbook, designed for a Willow Creek leadership retreat in the 1990s. A special note of thanks should go to Debbie Beise (now with the Lord), Cindi Salazar, Judson Poling, and Todd Wendorff for their contributions. Without their hard work and commitment, we would not have this valuable resource for leaders.

In the initial years of building a robust group ministry, many staff members played a strategic role to ensure success and shape our thinking. Thanks to Mark Weinert and Don Cousins, who developed our first disciple-making groups, and Jim Dethmer, Jon Wallace, Greg Hawkins, Brett Eastman, Judson Poling, and Marge Anderson, who helped lead us toward our initial vision to become a "church of groups."

I especially want to thank Russ Robinson for his friendship, partnership, and leadership as we shared many years building groups, training leaders, consulting with hundreds of churches, and writing together. We worked together during the great "build-up" era when almost twenty thousand adults, students, and kids found community in a small group.

In addition, I am so thankful for writing partner Greg Bowman and creative genius Dave Treat, two amazing leaders and group experts who designed conferences and equipped leaders worldwide with me at the Willow Creek Association (WCA). These guys are two of the best trainers I have ever seen in action.

And I want to thank the WCA and the Group Life Team, who have been working very hard to extend what we were learning about group life to the world for over ten years. This team includes Stephanie Walsh, Wendy Seidman, Stephanie Oakley, and the publishing team of Nancy Raney, Christine Anderson, and Doug Yonamine, and my very capable assistants Joan Oboyski and Cindy Martucci.

Pam Howell and Sherri Meyer brought the best of their skills in arts and production to help the WCA produce a top-notch Group Life Conference for many years. This platform allowed me to share ideas, inspire future leaders, and encourage Group Life Pastors around the world.

In more recent years, the Willow Group Life Team, the Group Life Pastors at Willow, and Ryan Chick, my partner in leadership development, all helped sharpen my thinking about groups and their essential role in making disciples.

Finally, I am very grateful to Bill Hybels and Jim Mellado, who provided the opportunity for me to help lead and shape the group life movement at the WCA and Willow Creek Church for eighteen years.

With a full heart,
Bill Donahue

BECOMING A BIBLICAL COMMUNITY

THAT THEY MIGHT BE ONE

We are created for community—for oneness—so that we can fully express the beauty, power, and image of God. His central focus for his creation is for us to become a community that enjoys his presence, demonstrates his love, and serves his purposes in the world, now and forever.

The Bible is clear: God never intended for us to be alone.

The Lord God said, "It is *not good* for the man to be alone. I will make a helper suitable for him."

Now the Lord God had formed out of the ground all the beasts of the field and all the birds of the air. He brought them to the man to see what he would name them; and whatever the man called each living creature, that was its name. So the man gave names to all the livestock, the birds of the air and all the beasts of the field.

But for Adam *no suitable helper* was found. So the Lord God caused the man to fall into a deep sleep; and while he was sleeping, he took one of the man's ribs and closed up the place with flesh. Then the Lord God made a woman from the rib he had taken out of the man, and he brought her to the man.

The man said,

"This is now bone of my bones
    and flesh of my flesh;
she shall be called 'woman,'
    for she was taken out of man."

For this reason a man will leave his father and mother and be united to his wife, and they will become one flesh.

The man and his wife were both naked, and they felt no shame.
    —Genesis 2:18–25 NIV, (italics added)

From the Garden of Eden to the present day, God has always intended for people to be in fellowship—community—with one another. Adam enjoyed full communion with God as Father, Son, and Spirit. Adam enjoyed a sin-free relationship with God, without the intrusion of pretense, fear, or suspicion to thwart genuine fellowship.

But it was *not good.*

Man had no equal, no partner, no being like him with whom to enjoy mutual fellowship. Adam had relational needs that God and the animals could not satisfy. Creation was less than Adam, something he would rule over and exercise authority over. The triune God was his master and leader, someone whose authority and power far transcended his.

He needed an equal. Not a servant, not a boss, not a slave, not a power broker. Someone like him.

I've heard people say that God is all you need in your life. Well, not according to God. Granted, there are times when all we *have* is God. We are alone, without friends or family to comfort, understand, or support us. In an ideal world—even in a fallen world—God has made it clear that aloneness is never preferred to oneness.

And the two shall become one.

Though this section of Scripture has clear implications for marriage, marriage is not the essential focus. God does not desire everyone to be married. But he wants his people to become one.

REFLECTION

What Is Oneness?

As you consider your role as a leader of a small group, what ideas come to mind as you think of oneness in your group? What might a group that experiences oneness look like?

THE TRINITY: THE FIRST SMALL GROUP

It should not surprise us that a shared life in community is the norm. Our triune God — Father, Son, and Holy Spirit — has always dwelled in perfect oneness. Yes, it is a mysterious oneness that we can never fully grasp. But the Bible is clear: each member of the Trinity is fully divine, and each is totally connected to the other in perfect relational harmony.

Some have referred to the relationship among members of the Trinity as "the shyness of the Trinity" because of the countercultural nature of their interaction. Remember, we must always be careful in describing such mysteries, but for a moment let's indulge the concept because it does reflect the character of our triune God.

The idea of shyness is used because though each is fully God and holds supreme power and authority, there is no haggling over who is greatest, most important, or most deserving of attention. Look at a few statements from the Bible.

- *The Father lifts up the Son.* "This is my Son, whom I have chosen; listen to him" (Luke 9:35). "The Father loves the Son and has placed everything in his hands" (John 3:35).
- *The Son lifts up the Father.* "Don't you believe that I [Jesus] am in the Father, and that the Father is in me? The words I say to you I do not speak on my own authority. Rather, it is the Father, living in me, who is doing his work" (John 14:10).
- *The Son lifts up the Spirit.* "I [Jesus] have much more to say to you, more than you can now bear. But when he, the Spirit of truth, comes, he will guide you into all the truth. He will not speak on his own; he will speak only what he hears, and he will tell you what is yet to come" (John 16:12 – 13).
- *The Spirit lifts up the Son.* "He [the Spirit] will glorify me [Jesus] because it is from me that he will receive what he will make known to you" (John 16:14).

These are a few examples of how the members of the Trinity — Father, Son, and Spirit — live as one God in three persons, without clamoring for attention and without competing for glory. God desires us to function in the same way. We are created in his image and are called to reflect the same kind of community that exists in the Trinity. We cannot do it without God's help in this sin-tainted world, but leaning on his power, we strive to reflect that reality.

The Trinity as "Small Group"

When we think of God as a small group of three persons sharing perfect community, what aspects of that image translate into your group? After all, we are far from perfect. So is there anything we see in God's nature that we can emulate in a small group of messed-up human beings?

JESUS: HIS GROUP AND HIS VISION FOR COMMUNITY

When we ponder what it takes to live in oneness, it's clear we are incapable. Most of us don't even know what that looks like. There are many examples of deep friendship and oneness in the stories of the Bible, but Jesus of Nazareth stands supreme as our model and guide for community.

Let's look at his practice here on earth and discover his passionate dream for community in the church. Look at these two sections of the Bible and take a few moments by yourself or with some other leaders to jot down some observations from Jesus's prayer for his followers.

A Prayer for Oneness (John 17:11 – 26)

I will remain in the world no longer, but they are still in the world, and I am coming to you. Holy Father, protect them by the power of your name, the name you gave me, so that they may be one as we are one. While I was with them, I protected them and kept them safe by that name you gave me. None has been lost except the one doomed to destruction so that Scripture would be fulfilled.

I am coming to you now, but I say these things while I am still in the world, so that they may have the full measure of my joy within them. I have given them your word and the world has hated them, for they are not of the world any more than I am of the world. My prayer is not that you take them out of the world but that you protect them from the evil one. They are not of the world, even as I am not of it. Sanctify them by the truth; your word is truth. As you sent me into the world, I have sent them into the world. For them I sanctify myself, that they too may be truly sanctified.

My prayer is not for them alone. I pray also for those who will believe in me through their message, that all of them may be one, Father, just as you are in me and I am in you. May they also be in us so that the world may believe that you have sent me. I have given them the glory that you gave me, that they may be one as we are one — I in them and you in me — so that they may be brought to complete unity. Then the world will know that you sent me and have loved them even as you have loved me.

Father, I want those you have given me to be with me where I am, and to see my glory, the glory you have given me because you loved me before the creation of the world.

Righteous Father, though the world does not know you, I know you, and they know that you have sent me. I have made you known to them, and will continue to make you known in order that the love you have for me may be in them and that I myself may be in them.

You might want to underline some key phrases or words or simply jot them down as you reflect on the questions in the following reflection.

REFLECTION

Jesus' Prayer for Community

1. As Jesus prays, how often does he repeat his desire that his followers be one? What does this tell you?

 continued on next page

2. From your reading of this prayer, why is oneness so important to Jesus? What does he say will be the result of our becoming one?

3. As you read through this section of Jesus's prayer, list some of the things he wants us to share with the Trinity. Some he has given us; some he asks the Father to provide. What are they?

Jesus longs for his followers to share in the fellowship of the Trinity — not simply to model it, not simply to understand it or to talk about it, but to *experience* it.

"May they be in us," he asks. Wow! He desires that we enter into the small group of the Trinity to experience what he experiences in that community. That is profound. So never think of yourself as "just a small group leader" in your church.

You are inviting others to join you in the fellowship of the Trinity!

Jesus and His Group (Mark 3:13 – 19)

One of Jesus's first priorities was to form a little community of disciples, similar to those of the other rabbis of his day. Communal learning was central to Jewish education, much unlike the individualized educational approaches in most Western cultures today. Even though Jesus's disciples were mostly uneducated and not typical rabbinic students, he wanted to be with them. He didn't just teach them; he spent a considerable amount of time in fellowship with them.

> Jesus went up on a mountainside and called to him those he wanted, and they came to him. He appointed twelve that they might be with him and that he might send them out to preach and to have authority to drive out demons. These are the twelve he appointed: Simon (to whom he gave the name Peter), James son of Zebedee and his brother John (to them he gave the name Boanerges, which means "sons of thunder"), Andrew, Philip, Bartholomew, Matthew, Thomas, James son of Alphaeus, Thaddaeus, Simon the Zealot and Judas Iscariot, who betrayed him.

We have to be careful about using Jesus's practice of group life with the twelve disciples as a standard model or system to be replicated today in our churches. Unless you are going on a three-year trip with twelve people of the same gender to mentor them for global ministry, you should rethink this approach.

We can learn much from Jesus's work with his disciples and certainly declare the priority this communal group life had in his ministry strategy. Following the disciples through the four gospels, we see that they did a lot together: eating, traveling, sleeping, teaching, healing, praying, listening, learning, failing, arguing, and scheming. They did much of life together as they observed the Master's interaction with people and sat under his teaching.

You might have much less time with your group. You might meet only a few times a month, plus make some spontaneous connections along the way (highly encouraged!). If you expect to have the same experience Jesus did, you will be frustrated.

Notice, Jesus chose the twelve "that they might be with him" before sending them out into ministry (a ministry that, compared with the group you are leading, likely had some unique qualities). But you can be with them as Jesus was with his little community.

The key to becoming a community is being together, as frequently as possible: at meals, church services, ministry gatherings, serving opportunities, prayer times, group meetings, those meeting-after-the-meeting moments, and when group members need extra help or care. Perhaps not everyone at every gathering, but as long as members are connecting throughout the week—by phone, by email, over coffee, chatting after a service—you will see the level of community increase.

Community in the New Testament

Community is a theme that runs throughout Scripture, even when we move beyond the Gospels. God has always been calling out a people for himself, beginning with Israel and continuing with the church. Even when the Jews were dispersed among enemy nations during times of captivity, they organized themselves into groups and ultimately formed synagogues (Jewish communities of worship and teaching) where they could serve others and live out their beliefs.

It was natural, therefore, for Jesus to develop a community of followers and for Paul, Peter, and other church planters to start new communities wherever they went as they proclaimed the gospel. These new communities began as small groups, just as Jesus had modeled with the twelve disciples (Mark 3:14; Luke 6:12 – 19).

Community-focused groups were an integral part of the early church strategy as well. They were small enough to allow members to minister to one another, use their spiritual gifts, and mature in the teachings of Christ. They were vibrant and life-giving communities where evangelism and service could take place as outsiders watched a loving and compassionate community in action. Small groups created a sense of oneness while also reaching a lost world for Christ.

These groups devoted themselves to the teaching of the apostles, to fellowship with one another, to practicing the Lord's Supper together, and to praying for one another. These new communities were characterized by mutuality, accountability, service, love, and evangelism.

Meeting in smaller groups allows each member to discover and use their spiritual gifts to serve other members in the body. Groups encourage and build up one another so that the body of Christ can be cared for and the world can be influenced through their good deeds.

BECOMING A COMMUNITY, ONE LIFE AT A TIME

If you are like me, you will want instant community. Have a few meetings, pray, read, laugh, cry, and *bang*—community!

Building community will take some time and effort. But you can count on this: the rewards are worth it. Remember the first time you connected deeply with some people who were on the same mission and seeking the same purposes in God's kingdom? Remember the thrill but also the work it took to come together and work through the relational snags that go along with every venture into oneness?

I do.

A group of about sixteen people wrecked my life in 1982. I was back in the Philadelphia area after college and after a year working in New York City. My banking job was an exciting new adventure, and I was enjoying the freedom that money and singleness afford a twenty-three-year-old male. I had just become a follower of Jesus but was in a church setting not conducive to much growth.

After a softball game one evening, a high school friend walked over from an adjacent field, and we quickly got reacquainted. We had played football together but had almost no interaction since those glory days five years earlier.

"Hey, I heard you are a Christian now," he remarked with a smirk.

"Uh . . . yes. Kind of a new thing in my life," I said, somewhat sheepishly, not knowing where conversations like this can go.

Then he smiled broadly and said, "Me too! It happened in college and really changed my life. Just heard you were back in town."

I remembered feeling relieved, no longer fearing that some kind of verbal persecution was coming my way.

"There are some others from our high school days who get together in a small group every week at my house. We pray, read the Bible, and have a lot of fun. Would you like to come?" he offered.

"Sure," I found myself saying, without a clue what a small group of Jesus people was like. "Just let me know when and where."

I had no idea that this group would transform my life, my career path, my relationships with women, and my adventure in church leadership.

But it did.

- I found real friends there, both men and women. (Before becoming a Christ follower, I hadn't done much to build friendships with women I didn't date.)
- I discovered a deep connection with God and with a few group members who made me feel safe but also accountable.
- I ended an unhealthy relationship with the woman I was dating.
- I left the bank to enter seminary for some ministry training.
- I began to understand how a small group becomes a community that transforms a life—forever.
- I moved from feeling separated from God's people to experiencing the oneness in Christian fellowship, the kind that God himself enjoys.

As you move through this material, my prayer is that you will find the same experience as a leader and as a participant in a group.

Let the adventure begin.

REFLECTION

Your Journey toward Community

As you think of your own journey into biblical community, what comes to mind? Was it smooth and simple? A hard road? Describe some of your reactions and what you have learned from experiences in groups and teams that might help you as you lead your small group.

ADDITIONAL RESOURCES

Gilbert Bilezikian, *Community 101* (Zondervan, 1997). A sound theological description of what oneness really looks like in life, faith, ministry, and leadership.

Dietrich Bonhoeffer, *Life Together* (HarperCollins, 1954). This classic by the persecuted WWII German pastor unpacks the reality and spiritual power of Christian community as we connect with others in Word, prayer, sacrament, and living together in the name of Jesus.

Larry Crabb, *The Safest Place on Earth* (W, 1999). Focuses on the environment that is most conducive to developing spiritual community with others.

Jean Vanier, *Community and Growth* (Paulist, 1989). A rich description of the various aspects of community life, written from the experience of the man who created the L'Arche communities for the disabled, across Canada. Written from a Catholic perspective.

Chapter 1

CLARIFYING YOUR PURPOSE

SPIRITUAL GROWTH AND COMMUNITY

Committed, authentic relationships have always been an essential component in the process of growth. This truth is a universal principle, not limited to the Christian life. Sociologists, psychologists, and health care workers agree that people who have strong relationships experience greater peace and joy, heal more quickly, and have fewer emotional health problems than those who live disconnected lives.

Community is at the core of the church, essential to both evangelism and discipleship. Howard Snyder writes, "At its most basic level the church is a community, not a hierarchy; an organism, not an organization (Mt. 18:20; Rom. 12:5 – 8; 1 Cor. 12; Eph. 4:1 – 16; 1 Pet. 4:10 – 11)" (*The Community of the King*, p. 73).

Later he adds, "Many churches do not share the gospel effectively because their communal experience of the gospel is too weak and tasteless to be worth sharing.... But where Christian fellowship demonstrates the gospel, believers come alive and sinners get curious and want to know what the secret is. So true Christian community (*koinonia*) becomes both the basis and the goal of evangelism.... The community is the only effective school for discipleship. For these reasons, building true *koinonia* is an indispensable link in the life cycle of church growth" (p. 147).

Therefore if we expect change to occur in people's lives, the community life of the church must be central, the epicenter of both the work of the Spirit and the transformational power of the Word.

The church, of course, has its roots in the Old Testament promises to Abraham, whose family was the first community to live out God's purpose for the world as a blessing to all nations. Later, as Israel came into being through Jacob, families became a central force for growth and life, followed closely by clans and tribes. Communal life flourished through these relational structures, which provided security, support during challenging times, strength in numbers, and the means of training up children in the ways of God.

"ONE ANOTHERS" OF THE NEW TESTAMENT

A new community in Christ was birthed in Acts 2, and from that time, a communal life not limited to family boundaries took precedence. Even under Jesus's teaching, it was clear that the nuclear family was not equivalent to the family of God, the church: "While Jesus was still talking to the crowd, his mother and brothers stood outside, wanting to speak to him. Someone told him, 'Your mother and brothers are standing outside, wanting to speak to you.' He replied to him, 'Who is my mother, and who are my brothers?' Pointing to his disciples, he said, 'Here are my mother and my brothers. For whoever does the will of my Father in heaven is my brother and sister and mother'" (Matt. 12:46–50).

This new emphasis on the church, and not the nuclear family or tribe, as the primary expression of community is scattered throughout the pages of the New Testament. A number of statements imply, if they do not directly teach, that it's in relationships—in groups, families, mission teams, friendships, and so on—that the faith is learned, practiced, and witnessed by the world.

Here are some of the most common examples.

- Be at peace with one another (Mark 9:50).
- Love one another (John 13:34).
- Be devoted to one another (Rom. 12:10).
- Honor one another (Rom. 12:10).
- Live in harmony with one another (Rom. 12:16).
- Stop passing judgment on one another (Rom. 14:13).
- Accept one another (Rom. 15:7).
- Instruct one another (Rom. 15:14).
- Greet one another (Rom. 16:16).
- Serve one another (Gal. 5:13).
- Carry one another's burdens (Gal. 6:2).
- Be patient, bearing with one another in love (Eph. 4:2).
- Be kind and compassionate to one another (Eph. 4:32).
- Forgive one another (Eph. 4:32).
- Speak to one another with psalms, hymns, and spiritual songs (Eph. 5:19).
- Submit to one another out of reverence for Christ (Eph. 5:21).
- In humility consider others better than yourselves (Phil. 2:3).

- Teach one another (Col. 3:16).
- Admonish one another (Col. 3:16).
- Encourage one another (1 Thess. 4:18).
- Build one another up (1 Thess. 5:11).
- Spur one another on toward love and good deeds (Heb. 10:24).
- Do not slander one another (James 4:11).
- Don't grumble against one another (James 5:9).
- Confess your sins to one another (James 5:16).
- Pray for one another (James 5:16).
- Clothe yourselves with humility toward one another (1 Peter 5:5).

Imagine your group fleshing out these "one anothers" as you live the way of Jesus. Imagine what would happen around you. Imagine how families and workplaces would be different, how neighborhoods and schools would be transformed, how skeptics and critics might have their hearts opened to the gospel.

Just imagine!

REFLECTION

Relational Discipleship

Take a few moments to ponder the connection between spiritual growth in Christ and our need for relationships. If you or your group got serious about this biblical idea, what might the future look like for all of you? How might this change the way you understand and pursue discipleship?

Since relationships help the body grow toward maturity in Christ (Eph. 4:16), your group's mission must focus on making disciples in the context of community. Whether your group is made up of spiritual seekers or newer followers of Christ or lifelong Christians, consider your mission to be the spiritual formation of disciples.

WHAT IS A DISCIPLE (FOLLOWER) OF JESUS?

Before crafting a mission statement, it's good to discuss what it means to be a disciple of Christ. The Bible gives us no clear definition of a disciple in a single verse or paragraph. Much of the Bible, of course, describes what the life of a follower of Jesus looks like. Many churches and parachurch organizations have tried to define *discipleship* or *disciple* so that people in their churches or ministries are clear about their goal. Such definitions are often very helpful, as long as it is made clear that they are only attempts to create a general description, not an exhaustive definition, of the characteristics of a follower of Jesus.

In the Bible, disciples came in all shapes and sizes, with different backgrounds, gifts, experiences, and levels of spiritual maturity. Some gave their lives for Christ, but some failed under pressure. Some followed only for a while to get their needs met, then left when Jesus's teaching or call to commitment got too intense (John 6:60–71).

So your church or ministry's description of a disciple needs to be a good framework on which to build a way of life in the kingdom of God. Be cautious when you define what a disciple is. Definitions can easily be used to judge people or to wrongly deny someone opportunities for leadership or development. Strive instead to describe the heart, beliefs, attitudes, and activities of followers of Jesus that we can all aspire to as we "spur one another on toward love and good deeds" (Heb. 10:24).

The focus of making disciples of Jesus should be on the "of Jesus" part. The focus is not on our systems, definitions, processes, and measurements, as helpful and necessary as those things may be. Rather, it is on observing Jesus's character, mission, and life, encouraging one another to trust and follow him fully. "A student is not above his teacher, nor a servant above his master. It is enough for the student to be *like his teacher*, and the servant *like his master*" (Matt. 10:24–25 NIV, italics added).

We are called to be like him. Never lose sight of that goal. A disciple is a follower of Jesus Christ who seeks to obey his teachings and to imitate his way of life.

As much as possible, make sure your description aligns with the description provided by the leadership of your church or ministry. To the degree that you can adapt that description to your group, do so. Work with your leadership to ensure your group is aligned with your church or ministry.

Take some time to jot down some characteristics—beliefs, actions, character—of a follower of Jesus. Don't worry about naming every possible trait and commitment. That would cover most of the New Testament! Write down a few core concepts, or simply copy your church's description, if one exists.

REFLECTION

Description of a Disciple

A follower or disciple of Jesus is:

Now that you have an idea of what a disciple is, let's look at your group's mission to work together as a community to become more fully devoted followers of Jesus.

MISSION

What are we doing together?

A clear mission is key to your group's success. Every mission has a few key components. The larger and more complex the group, the more detailed the mission needs to be so that everyone understands it. Every group needs focus, but not every group needs as much detail.

In the sidebar on pages 29–31 is an exercise to work through as you develop your group's mission. It's fine if you cannot complete all of it now. You might want to work through this exercise as a group, gaining clarity and consensus as you move along. Depending on the nature and focus of your group, you may even decide to skip parts of it.

DEVELOPING YOUR GROUP MISSION

1. What characteristics do we expect of disciples in our group? (The purpose of this exercise is to gain perspective and set some goals for development, not to compile a legalistic checklist.)

   Beliefs:

continued on next page

Attitudes:

Commitments:

Spiritual Practices:

Actions and Service:

2. How will our group help the disciple-making process?

Format of Meetings:

Use of the Bible:

Use of Discussion Materials:

Role of Prayer:

Environment to Create (safety, respect, honor, and so on):

Activities or Other Gatherings:

Crafting Your Mission Statement

The goal is not to take everything you just wrote in the sidebar and cram it into a mission statement. Instead, use what you have written to clarify what your focus will be. Not every group can be everything for everyone.

The key questions are, What is our unique mission as a group? Who are we and what are we going to try to do together for the next few months?

You can revise the mission statement every six months or so, depending on the needs and direction of your group.

The following steps can help you create your mission statement:

1. First, "determine your infinitive." An infinitive is a phrase that begins with the word *to*. The phrase you write may depend on what kind of group you are leading. (If you are not sure what kind of group you want to lead, see appendix 1, "Kinds of Small Groups," for ideas.) Some examples of infinitives:

   - To become
   - To create
   - To learn
   - To build
   - To experience
   - To serve
   - To empower
   - To discover
   - To practice

2. Next, write a "by means of" or "through" phrase that defines your process or approach to the mission. For example, "through Bible study and prayer" or "by practicing an authentic faith."

3. Finally, write a "so that" or "in order to" phrase. For example, a women's group might write: "in order to become Christ-centered mothers who can guide younger moms through the difficult months following childbirth." A group whose approach to its mission is through learning the core doctrines of the Christian faith might write: "so that we can discern truth from error and build confidence in our beliefs."

Sample Mission Statements

- "To create an environment characterized by grace, truth, and humility, so that our nonbelieving friends will discover the group as a safe place to share their lives and observe authentic Christlike love and relationships."
- "To challenge and support one another toward full devotion to Christ, by providing an environment for connection with God, authentic community, and spiritual formation."
- "To make disciples of Jesus Christ by equipping one another through engagement with Scripture, mutual accountability, holy living, and

sacrificial service to others, so that our families and communities will see Jesus's love in action."

REFLECTION

Writing Your Mission Statement

To:

By or through:

So that:

VALUES

Why are we gathering as a group? What do we believe about the environment we are creating in which to grow together?

Values are your underlying beliefs about your small group. They are not doctrinal beliefs but rather the firmly held principles that govern how you will function together, treat one another, and create an environment conducive to accomplishing your mission.

For example, an organization trains people to be effective classroom teachers because they hold a value: every student deserves a quality teacher. A recovery group uses the twelve-steps strategy because they hold a value: people need a safe, authentic community to provide the support essential to overcoming addictive behavior.

Most small groups have a set of fundamental values about group life. Here are a few.

Safety: Creating a place free of judgment and condemnation in order to build a foundation for trust.

Authenticity: Being real about pain, struggles, joys, hopes, dreams, fears, thoughts, and feelings. Avoiding pretense and putting on a false self to hide real issues and needs.

Care: Expressing concern and support to one another with words and actions.

Growth: A desire to make progress in life — spiritually, emotionally, and relationally.

Confidentiality: Promising not to talk to people outside the group about what people share and do in the group.

Respect: Honoring each person's right to have opinions and recognizing their dignity as a human being.

Later in this book, you will be guided through the process of setting ground rules — or "covenants," as some groups call them. This process includes naming and clarifying your core values.

For now, it is important that you begin thinking about values in light of your group's mission or purpose. As a leader, it is sometimes essential or even expected that you lead your group through the process of discussing its values together by having some ideas of your own. Starting with a blank slate and asking, "So what do you think our values should be?" is probably too open-ended of an approach for people.

REFLECTION

Writing Your Values List

Take a few moments to list five or six core values of your group, then define each one and prioritize them by placing numbers next to them. Remember, you will process these later with your group.

-
-
-
-
-

VISION

Where are we going together? What will it look like when we arrive?

If the mission (What are we doing?) is the itinerary for a trip, the vision (What does the destination look like?) is the travel brochure.

When my wife and I traveled to Italy for a speaking engagement, I was excited by the brochure, not the itinerary. Photographs of the majestic artwork and ancient ruins of Rome, Florence, and Capri, and of the romantic countryside surrounding those cities, created in me a desire to go to Italy. The itinerary—departure times, airline seats, hotel locations, travel dates, time spent in each city—was crucial to the success of the trip. But there was little there to inspire me.

When people asked, "Where are you going in Italy?" we didn't answer, "We're flying to Rome on a 757 jet in seats 23A and 23B for eight hours and forty-two minutes, landing on a runway and then getting our bags, and then ..." We said, "After a few days in Rome at the Coliseum and seeing all the ancient sites, we're headed to Florence for a beautiful lunch on the veranda of a villa overlooking a vineyard! Then we're going to see Michelangelo's *David* at the Academia Gallery ..."

Vision inspires and motivates. It provides a picture of a preferred future, something you are moving toward together, something you want to become as you accomplish the mission.

Completing a mission solves a problem; pursuing a vision fulfills a longing. One moves the hands; the other stirs the heart.

Your group might be "studying a parenting curriculum to learn biblical principles for raising our kids," but that is not the vision. That is the mission. The vision might be, "To become caring, godly parents raising our children with tender discipline, bold love, and creative, fun-filled engagement."

Vision Questions

Before you work through the following questions: Chapter 4 of this book presents material which is to be used by the whole group. *But at this time, you will be thinking* only about your vision *and will be working alone on the material in the following section. When you meet with your group, use this material and the information in chapter 4 to help the entire group embrace a vision. If you are in a training class at the moment and are not leading a group, the following material will help you get started.*

Here are a few questions to prompt the development of your vision. Keeping in mind your group's mission and values, take a few minutes to dream about the future. What might it be like when God works through and in your group to accomplish your mission?

1. What do we want to become? What kind of group?
2. What will our lives look like if we complete the mission?
3. How will our relationships feel?
4. What kind of community will we experience?
5. How will others be different if we reach them with our mission?
6. How will the culture or workplace or neighborhood look when we are successful?
7. How might our families or marriages or dating relationships feel?

Vision statements are generally shorter than mission statements. Your vision statement might be something like "To be a place where no one stands alone" or "To become fully devoted fathers with passion for our kids" or "To create a neighborhood where the love of Jesus impacts every family's story."

REFLECTION

Writing Your Vision Statement

Write your vision statement here:

PUTTING IT ALL TOGETHER

Now that you have drafted your mission statement, values list, and vision statement, use the following sidebar to summarize your work so you can easily refer to it in the months and years ahead.

THE PURPOSE OF OUR GROUP: SPIRITUAL GROWTH

Our Mission:

Our Values:

Our Vision:

ADDITIONAL RESOURCES

George Barna, *The Power of Vision* (Regal, 2009). The fact that this resource is in its third edition testifies to its impact and usefulness for shaping and communicating vision.

Bill Donahue and Russ Robinson, *Building a Life-Changing Small Group Ministry* (Zondervan, 2012). The early sections of this book describe the philosophy and theology of group life and making disciples.

Will Mancini, *Church Unique* (Jossey-Bass, 2008). Helps churches think creatively about their unique vision. Mancini's "Vision Frame" is a great approach to shaping vision.

Greg Ogden, *Discipleship Essentials* (InterVarsity, 2007). Provides a clear structured process for guiding a cluster of people along a discipleship journey.

Chapter 2

SHARPENING YOUR LEADERSHIP

WHAT KIND OF LEADER DO I NEED TO BECOME?

We often say, "Leadership is the whole ball game." We know from Scripture and experience that little ministry is sustained for long without a God-inspired leader to rally people to the cause and encourage them along the way. Look at them—Abraham, Deborah, David, Peter, Paul, Phoebe, Lydia, and the rest—and you will see that God works through leaders to shepherd and mobilize his people. We're not trying to elevate leaders unnecessarily, because leaders are servants.

Small groups need called and qualified leaders. We want to help you understand the incredible privileges—and responsibilities—associated with leadership. We want to help you gain clarity about what a small group leader is and what the leader's ministry looks like, and then show you how to do some self-leadership that will keep you growing and effective.

It's a good thing to aspire to leadership, but we must always do a quick heart check. As we consider the kind of leader you need to become, let's check your motivation for leading others.

Appropriate Motives for Leadership

Serve Christ

"Whatever you do, work at it with all your heart, as working for the Lord, not for men, since you know that you will receive an inheritance from the Lord as a reward. It is the Lord Christ you are serving" (Col. 3:23–24 NIV).

Bear fruit in your life

"This is to my Father's glory, that you bear much fruit, showing yourselves to be my disciples" (John 15:8).

Keep watch over (shepherd) others

"Keep watch over yourselves and all the flock of which the Holy Spirit has made you overseers. Be shepherds of the church of God, which he bought with his own blood" (Acts 20:28).

Be an example to the body

"Be shepherds of God's flock that is under your care, serving as overseers—not because you must, but because you are willing, as God wants you to be; not greedy for money, but eager to serve; not lording it over those entrusted to you, but being examples to the flock. And when the Chief Shepherd appears, you will receive the crown of glory that will never fade away" (1 Peter 5:2–4 NIV).

Use your gifts to serve others

"It was he who gave some to be apostles, some to be prophets, some to be evangelists, and some to be pastors and teachers, to prepare God's people for works of service, so that the body of Christ may be built up until we all reach unity in the faith and in the knowledge of the Son of God and become mature, attaining to the whole measure of the fullness of Christ" (Eph. 4:11–13 NIV).

Communicate the message of reconciliation

" … that God was reconciling the world to himself in Christ, not counting men's sins against them. And he has committed to us the message of reconciliation. We are therefore Christ's ambassadors, as though God were making his appeal through us. We implore you on Christ's behalf: Be reconciled to God. God made him who had no sin to be sin for us, so that in him we might become the righteousness of God" (2 Cor. 5:19–21 NIV).

Wrong Motives for or Hindrances to Leadership
Self-exaltation

"Let another praise you, and not your own mouth; someone else, and not your own lips" (Prov. 27:2 NIV).

To feel important or gain prestige

"We speak as men approved by God to be entrusted with the gospel. We are not trying to please men but God, who tests our hearts. You know we never used flattery, nor did we put on a mask to cover up greed—God is our witness. We were not looking for praise from men, not from you or anyone else" (1 Thess. 2:4–6 NIV).

Because someone pressured you

"Be shepherds of God's flock that is under your care, serving as over-seers—not because you must, but because you are willing, as God wants you to be" (1 Peter 5:2 NIV).

Having a short fuse or exhibiting outbursts of anger

James tells us that human anger does not achieve the righteousness of God (James 1:19–20). God's work is accomplished by one who listens attentively, speaks only when necessary, and is slow to anger. Leaders manage their anger or channel anger appropriately. Anger is to be put aside or properly managed (Gal. 5:20; Eph. 4:31; Col. 3:8).

Unconfessed sin

We are commanded to confess our sins. John says, "If we confess our sins, he is faithful and just and will forgive us our sins and purify us from all unrighteousness" (1 John 1:9). Any sin that has control of us (Rom. 6:16) must be confessed and brought under the lordship of Christ (Acts 2:38). Outstanding sin that is not dealt with appropriately could disqualify a leader.

Biblical error or false teaching

Paul warned Timothy to watch for false teachers who lead people away from the faith: "For the time will come when men will not put up with sound doctrine. Instead, to suit their own desires, they will gather around them a great number of teachers to say what their itching ears want to hear. They will turn their ears away from the truth and turn aside to myths" (2 Tim. 4:3–4).

BIBLICAL LEADERSHIP: FOUR BASIC PRINCIPLES

1. Leaders Are Christ-Centered

Every believer needs to connect daily with Christ, but this is especially true with group leaders. From Christ we draw strength and hope, confidence and cleansing. You lead best from an inner life that is growing and developing intimacy with Christ. In so doing, you can call your group toward the same commitment. Paul said, "Follow my example, as I follow the example of Christ" (1 Cor. 11:1). Spend time in God's presence and fill your deep longings for him when you suffer or experience brokenness (Ps. 42:1).

Christ-centered leaders become Christlike leaders. Leaders must pay attention to the heart—to integrity and character. Proverbs 4:23 exhorts the wise person to "watch over your heart with all diligence, for from it flow the springs of life" (NASB). In Matthew 12:35, Jesus challenges the heart of the Pharisees, saying, "The good man brings good things out of the good stored up in him, and the evil man brings evil things out of the evil stored up in him" (NIV).

People need to be able to trust their leader, the way they trust Christ. Leadership is impossible apart from trust. Being truthful and trustworthy contributes to a leader's character; when trust is broken, it is difficult to restore. Paul encouraged a young leader, Timothy, to "set an example for the believers in speech, in life, in love, in faith and in purity" (1 Tim. 4:12 NIV). He wanted him to maintain his integrity and to model the Christian life for the rest of the church.

Like Christ, leaders will be tempted. You must work to protect your heart from thoughts, actions, and attitudes that will corrupt or harden it. Be willing to engage in self-examination and peer examination. Ask people where you have character weaknesses and strengths; evaluate your own heart before God and with Scripture.

2. Leaders Are Servants

In Scripture, ministry and service are synonymous with leadership. The one who is not willing to serve is not fit to lead. Jesus set the standard when he said, "Even the Son of Man did not come to be served, but to serve, and to give his life as a ransom for many" (Mark 10:45). Often leadership—even Christian leadership—is patterned after business or political models, which emphasize the organizational component of leadership.

Look at the biblical pattern, and you get a different perspective. Leaders are referred to as shepherds who guide and serve the flock, caring for and developing those around them. Leaders pick up the servant's towel (John 13:1–17) and model the life and leadership of Christ.

Jesus said, "Whoever serves me must follow me; and where I am, my servant also will be. My Father will honor the one who serves me" (John 12:26).

3. Leaders Are Shepherds

Some of you have the spiritual gift of leadership; some of you are gifted to teach; others have mercy gifts and discernment gifts. Regardless of your gift mix, all small group leaders function as shepherds. Jesus called himself the Good Shepherd—one who is concerned about the health of the flock.

The term *shepherd* is not familiar today in most Western cultures. *Leader* or *guide* are more common labels.

Jesus used *shepherds* to describe the role of leaders, and we want to learn what the Bible says about this breed of leadership. There were other leaders in Jesus's day — in government, education, religious and social life — but he chose a rather lowly (and smelly) role to describe his own leadership and that of the ones who were to guide the people in his church.

Christ characterized his ministry in this way: "I am the good shepherd; I know my sheep and my sheep know me" (John 10:14). He was willing to lay down his life for the sake of the cause, for the love of the community. What does that look like in small group terms? Chapter 6 has more resources and information to help you answer that question and to show you how to create an environment of mutual care in your group.

4. Leaders Work Together

No one leads alone! That has been a mantra of mine for some time. Jesus called his followers into a community in order to develop them as leaders.

When it was time for them to participate in ministry, Jesus sent them out in groups (the twelve apostles in Matthew 10) and in pairs (the seventy-two emerging leaders in Luke 10:1). When needs were prevalent in the early community, teams were appointed to provide gift-based servant leadership (Acts 6).

At every point in the church's development, the leadership structure included a plurality of leaders. Paul appointed elders to lead a church once it was established in any city, and he often worked with one or more partners in his ministry efforts, including men and women in his leadership circle (see Rom. 16).

A small group leader should model such leadership by working with one or more apprentices or fellow leaders, serving together in community. By doing so, he or she shares leadership and avoids the temptation to become the only one with a leadership role. Apprenticing will be discussed fully in chapter 3.

BASIC QUALIFICATIONS FOR SMALL GROUP LEADERSHIP

Who is fit to lead a small group? Your church may already have guidelines to answer this question, and it's likely you already meet them or are on your way to that goal, or you wouldn't be working through this material.

There are usually two approaches to determining who is qualified. Which approach is taken depends on one's view of what a small group should be. People who view the small group as an all-encompassing disciple-making machine want it to be led by the apostle Paul or someone like Priscilla, a leader in the early church. In these people's view, groups must study the Bible, train members for the entire Christian life, challenge them to missionary service, and cover every category of Christian theology. On the other extreme are people who think anyone who has a pulse and can fog a mirror can lead a group. Wisdom dictates that we must somehow communicate the significance and seriousness of guiding people toward growth in Christ, while also realizing that even gifted leaders need time to acquire all the skills and discernment for effective leading.

There are at least some common qualifications you should consider when taking on the leadership challenge or developing potential leaders. These qualifications are essential for fulfilling a biblical role of leadership. Again, I emphasize that your church will likely bring much clarity to this, so please consider the material to follow as recommendations. Take the time to discuss this with your church leadership in order to align with the mission and purposes of your church.

1. *I recognize the Bible as the true Word of God and as authoritative in my life.* Scripture is essential for living life in Christ and in his community, the church. It has authority because it is the teachings and stories of the triune God through the ages. God is our ultimate authority, and we submit to him. We obey his Word because it comes from him, was given to us by him through his Spirit, and has the power to transform lives.

2. *I am in a personal, growing relationship with Jesus Christ, my Savior and Lord.* A leader in the body of Christ is a member of that body. The only way to be a member of the body of Christ is to trust Christ for salvation and for ongoing discipleship. He has forgiven our sins and calls us to love him and obey his teaching.

   By his grace, and with the help of his Spirit, his Word, and wisdom from others in the body of Christ, I am seeking to grow toward maturity. A leader is not expected to be *perfect* but is expected to be an active *participant* in pursuit of the kind of life Jesus calls us toward.

3. *I agree to submit to and be accountable to the leaders of my church, whom God has placed in roles of responsibility and authority in his church.* It is a general principle from the Bible that we are to honor, respect, and follow people in authority over us, particularly in the church. This is not intended to convey some blind allegiance to man's authority,

nor to assume that every leader is worthy of the respect and honor due him or her.

Men and women with leadership gifts have been given roles by God—as apostles, prophets, evangelists, pastors, and teachers—to build up the body of Christ. Some of these people, along with others with other gifts, have been chosen for leadership positions in the church, such as elders, deacons, and board or council members (each church uses different terminology).

These leaders are responsible to shepherd God's people toward maturity, to protect the church, and to fulfill God's call for each local church to expand God's kingdom on earth.

4. *I have the emotional capacity and discernment to guide others in a group process.* This implies that a potential leader is willing to make the time for, and reserve some energy to give to, group leadership. The capacity to lead others is compromised when there are great stresses on a potential leader (relational breakdown in marriage or family, addictions and sin patterns that are not being addressed, exhaustion or too many other life commitments).

   In addition, there is a level of relational discernment that requires some emotional intelligence. You must have the capacity to relate to people in healthy, productive ways, being able to discern when and how to engage with others (provide care, show love, express concern, confront destructive attitudes, and so on) as the situation requires.

   You are *not* a professional counselor or relationship expert—just someone who has a healthy understanding of relationships and has a general awareness of how to deal with your group with grace and truth.

To sum up, if you do not believe the Bible, do not have a growing walk with Jesus, will not or cannot be accountable to reasonable, godly leaders in the church, and/or cannot bring relational discernment and energy to a leadership role, then perhaps you should hit the pause button for becoming a leader at this point in time. Work with your church to determine areas for growth and development that will help you qualify in the future. Your personal growth and relationship to Jesus and his church are more important than your filling a leadership role!

In addition to these qualifications, your church or ministry may have other expectations. For example, some churches require you to have been a believer for at least one year, or to have been in a small group for a period of time, or to attend classes or training, or to become a church member. These are all reasonable, and they vary from church to church.

REFLECTION

1. Am I willing to shape my leadership around the four principles of biblical leadership?

Be Christ-centered	Y	N
View myself as a shepherd	Y	N
Maintain the posture of a servant	Y	N
Share leadership with others	Y	N

2. Do I possess the qualifications for leadership as outlined earlier and as described by the leaders of my church? If not, am I willing to grow in areas they recommend so that I can take a leadership role someday?   Y   N

CORE LEADERSHIP PRACTICES

In every profession, area of expertise, or skill, there are core practices essential to achieving a level of competence and success. A young baseball player must learn to throw, catch, hit, and run the bases. An emerging violinist must learn finger positions, practice scales, understand musical terminology, and have an ear for tone and pitch. Bankers must become experts at attracting new customers, make quality loans, and manage cash effectively, or there will be no bank.

What, then, are the core practices of a group leader? Every effective and transformational small group leader does four things—listen, learn, love, and lead.

1. Listen

I asked a church leader and trained Christian psychologist what he would teach a room filled with small group leaders if he had them for an entire day. He wasted no time answering.

"I would train them to listen!" he said with great conviction.

"And what about the rest of the day?" I asked.

"That's it," he said to me as if speaking to a small child who had just asked how to build a nuclear submarine. "We'd spend *the whole day* on listening."

The whole day? Now I was listening!

Listening is essential in any relationship, especially in marriages, families, and small groups. Groups, in particular, must navigate a more complex relational environment, because of the sheer numbers of people involved, often six to fifteen. A leader must practice the art and skill of active listening, so that he or she can fully engage with God and group members.

The Bible affirms that listening—really listening—is the mark of a wise person.

"He who answers before listening—that is his folly and his shame" (Prov. 18:13 NIV).

"Even fools are thought wise if they keep silent, and discerning if they hold their tongues" (Prov. 17:28).

Listening doesn't simply mean not talking, though that can help if you tend to interrupt and live in the world of Proverbs 18:13. Active listening means asking questions, making observations, feeding back information to the speaker, and seeking greater understanding of what is being discussed.

Active listening involves not only what you hear but also what you say. This means engaging with the speaker, setting aside your personal agenda, and keeping yourself from distracting thoughts (particularly about what you're going to say next!). Here are some tips for active listening.

What you say

1. Invite comments from the group.
2. Empathize with people's emotions.
3. Explore their statements, seeking more information.
4. Clarify what has been said.

What you hear

1. *Verbal* (the content of what is said). Sometimes we are so interested in what we are about to say that we fail to hear the simple facts in a discussion. As you listen, focus on people's names, events, dates, and other specific information being shared.
2. *Nonverbal* (how the content is expressed). Here you are listening for congruity, that is, do the nonverbal messages match the verbal messages? Listen for this in three areas:

   - *Facial expressions.* When someone says, "I'm okay," does their facial expression communicate, "I'm a little sad"?
   - *Tone of voice.* Listen for tones of sarcasm, anger, sadness, enthusiasm, hesitancy, fear, and so on.

- *Body movements and posture.* Are arms and legs crossed and closed? Are people fidgety or relaxed? Does their posture indicate interest or boredom? Remember, you can "hear" a lot just by watching people's actions.

The following table will help by comparing active listening with a passive form of listening that is not really engaged. As a leader, how would you rate yourself?

Listening Skills
Passive versus Active Listening

	Passive Listening	Active Listening
Attitude	Rejecting, critical. *"I'm really not interested."*	Receptive, accepting. *"I really want to hear."*
Focus	Me — what I want to say. *"What do I think?"*	Other person — what others are saying. *"What does he mean?"*
Response	Express what I've been thinking. *"I think you should ..."*	Clarify first what I've heard the other person say. *"You think ..." "Do you feel ..."*
Message	What you said isn't important. *"I didn't really hear what you said."*	I heard both the feeling and the need in the message. *"I heard what you said."*
Results	Speaker experiences frustration, anger. *Listener communicates, "I don't care."*	Speaker is willing to compromise or tell more. *Listener says, "I care about what you said."*

This would be great material to review with your group, especially if it's just starting.

Favorite phrases used by active listeners

- Please tell me more about that.
- Let me see if I understood what you just said.
- Could you repeat that last idea — I really want to hear that clearly.
- As you said those words, it sounded as though you might be (happy, sad, angry, excited, tender, confused, scared, reluctant, and so on), and I wanted to see if that is accurate.
- As you describe that situation, I cannot help but feel (X), and I wondered if you felt the same way.

- That must have been (hard, easy, exciting, awkward, challenging, painful, and so on) for you.
- Am I understanding you correctly?
- Is there anything you were hoping I would understand or feel or decide as a result of our conversation?

The impact of really listening

- Others feel and believe you really care.
- Others respect you.
- Others view you as safe and a person in whom they can confide.
- Others in the group learn to listen as they watch and hear you.
- You earn the right to lead people to new areas of growth.
- You are able to confront difficult people and situations with grace and skill.
- You really learn about people—their thoughts, emotions, needs, concerns, hopes.
- You gain insight for how and where to guide a discussion.
- You discover how to express care and love to others.
- You help seekers and skeptics open up and express contrary points of view.
- Trust grows.
- Relationships deepen.
- People bring hidden parts of life to the surface.

By listening well, you build a foundation for the remaining three core practices of a group leader.

REFLECTION

Improving My Listening

I need to grow in my ability to be an active listener by:

2. Learn

Jesus wanted every follower—and particularly every leader—to be a learner. At the end of his most decisive and provocative teaching, the Sermon on the Mount, he makes these challenging comments: "Everyone who hears these words of mine and puts them into practice is like a wise man who built his house on the rock. The rain came down, the streams rose, and the winds blew and beat against that house; yet it did not fall, because it had its foundation on the rock. But everyone who hears these words of mine and does not put them into practice is like a foolish man who built his house on sand. The rain came down, the streams rose, and the winds blew and beat against that house, and it fell with a great crash" (Matt. 7:24–27).

Someone has said, "When you are through learning, you're through!" This is so true! Leaders are learners—and learning will help you maintain your leadership edge.

Paul wanted Timothy to work at his teaching so that he would be a competent communicator of God's truth. He said, "Do your best to present yourself to God as one approved, a worker who does not need to be ashamed and who correctly handles the word of truth" (2 Tim. 2:15). Being good at your ministry really counts.

Becoming competent means pursuing personal development and skill training for the ministry in which you serve. Basic small group skills are necessary regardless of the kind of group you lead, but many types of groups require specific training as well. Identify your core abilities and then work hard to sharpen those competencies while acquiring additional leadership skills.

People know that leaders are far from perfect. We sin, make mistakes, and have flaws that all humans share. They do expect us to be in the game and growing in our character, skills, and knowledge.

"David shepherded them with integrity of heart; with skillful hands he led them" (Ps. 78:72).

David failed. He struggled and labored to lead God's people—his flock—with integrity and with skill. We all know he wasn't perfect. Yet he was in the game. His life and leadership were characterized by faith, a heart for God, and a willingness to repent and grow. David was a learner. Look at Psalm 78 again, a few verses earlier.

"He chose David his servant and took him from the sheep pens; from tending the sheep he brought him to be the shepherd of his people Jacob, of Israel his inheritance" (Ps. 78:70–71).

God used David's skill and experience from other aspects of his life for spiritual leadership in Israel.

So what have you learned so far about leading? About group life? What skills do you possess, and what skills do you need to master?

Take a few moments to complete the following checklist to see where you might need additional growth or training.

Skill Assessment	I Need Development	I Am Strong
• Vision casting	☐	☐
• Raising up an apprentice leader	☐	☐
• Modeling accountability	☐	☐
• Planning a meeting	☐	☐
• Asking good questions	☐	☐
• Leading discussions	☐	☐
• Using the Bible in groups	☐	☐
• Choosing curriculum	☐	☐
• Opening a meeting creatively	☐	☐
• Using a variety of prayers in a group	☐	☐
• Evaluating progress	☐	☐
• Providing care between meetings	☐	☐
• Building relationships	☐	☐
• Praying for members	☐	☐
• Resolving conflict	☐	☐
• Meeting special needs	☐	☐
• Serving with others	☐	☐
• Practicing listening skills	☐	☐
• Promoting growth	☐	☐
• Adding new members	☐	☐
• Breaking into subgroups for prayer and discussion	☐	☐

In addition to your own assessment of your skills, ask the people who recruited you as a leader, or ask some close, trusted friends or ministry partners, to assess you on the same topics. Consider asking members of the group you were in before you became a leader. Peer evaluation and honest feedback will help you design a growth strategy for your leadership.

Determine to learn about group members—about their lives, families, passions, gifts, dreams, and so on. It will help you pray for them and serve them. Regularly attending church services and classes will also help you learn about the Bible and the core doctrines of the faith so that you can lead with increasing confidence and wisdom.

As you become a learner—in every area—you will discover more about God and your group. You'll also learn about yourself, especially about your gifts and where best to use them. Perhaps you are frustrated in leadership because you're in the wrong ministry (working with kids, for example, instead of adults). In 1 Corinthians 12:4–7 it is clear that each Christ follower has a gift (or has gifts) for building up the body of Christ. Your gifts—combined with unique God-given abilities, personality, and experiences—will flourish in some ministry areas and be stunted in others. It's important for every leader to know the kind of small group ministry that best aligns with how God made them.

Take time to assess whether you would fit best with adults or children, working at a task or providing care to the hurting, leading a study group or a mission project. Each of these is accomplished in community and needs gifted leaders to bring their best to the effort. Your church leadership team can recommend some assessment tools and processes to help you, and you might have already completed such a process. If not, make that an area for development. If you know what your gifts, experiences, and passions are, fill in the following reflection to capture this information here.

REFLECTION

Knowing My Gifts, Experiences, and Areas of Passion

My spiritual gifts are:

My leadership experience reveals I have strengths in:

continued on next page

My passion and desire is to be involved in a ministry or leadership role that serves:

3. Love

You will never earn the right to fully lead people you do not love. Caring, trusting relationships form the foundation for every vibrant community. Leaders set the pace here, following Christ's example (John 13:1). Love for God, for the church, for the small group, and for the lost are trademarks of growing leaders. People tend to receive truth more readily—including correction or rebuke—when you genuinely care for them.

Listening will help you understand people and their needs. Learning will help you acquire the skills and knowledge and character to become a leader who can guide others. Without *love*, it all amounts to nothing. A familiar passage should come to mind.

> If I speak in the tongues of men and of angels, but have not love, I am only a resounding gong or a clanging cymbal. If I have the gift of prophecy and can fathom all mysteries and all knowledge, and if I have a faith that can move mountains, but have not love, I am nothing. If I give all I possess to the poor and surrender my body to the flames, but have not love, I gain nothing.
>
> Love is patient, love is kind. It does not envy, it does not boast, it is not proud. It is not rude, it is not self-seeking, it is not easily angered, it keeps no record of wrongs. Love does not delight in evil but rejoices with the truth. It always protects, always trusts, always hopes, always perseveres.
>
> Love never fails. But where there are prophecies, they will cease; where there are tongues, they will be stilled; where there is knowledge, it will pass away. For we know in part and we prophesy in part, but when perfection comes, the imperfect disappears. When I was a child, I talked like a child, I thought like a child, I reasoned like a child. When I became a man, I put childish ways behind me. Now we see but a poor reflection as in a mirror; then we shall see face to face. Now I know in part; then I shall know fully, even as I am fully known.

And now these three remain: faith, hope and love. But the greatest of these is love.

—1 Corinthians 13 NIV

I have often made it a point to understand the love languages of people in groups I have led. It has helped me understand—not label—people so that I and others in the group can wisely express affection, care, and concern in meaningful ways.

Gary Chapman lists these areas of focus in the book *The Five Love Languages*:

- Words of affirmation
- Appropriate touch
- Giving gifts
- Acts of service
- Time spent together

Get to know your people and genuinely express bold love to them. In most cases, they will eagerly follow your leadership. If you currently lead a group or have a good idea of who some of your group members might be, then, using the following table, take a moment to check your understanding of their love languages.

Group Member	Love Language	What would communicate love to this group member?

Leaders are lovers.

Jesus made that clear when he reinstated Peter after Peter denied him during his trial. Three times, Peter had claimed no relationship to Jesus. Later he was ashamed. But Jesus—and this is crucial for all leaders—Jesus is in the business of redeeming the repentant! He loves it when prodigals come home—especially prodigal leaders! When our hearts are rightly aligned with his, even after failures, mistakes, and sins we are ashamed of, he is willing to restore and reposition you as a leader. God is in the business of turning leadership failures—from Abraham and Moses to Mary Magdalene and Paul—into fruit.

Aren't we all very glad about that timeless truth!

When Jesus restored Peter to his role and prominence as a leader in the church, he made one important demand of him. He wanted to affirm that any future leadership role for Peter would require a leader who loves the "sheep"—the people we meet every day, certainly fellow believers but also those not yet in the fold.

Leaders are first and foremost lovers!

> When they had finished eating, Jesus said to Simon Peter, "Simon son of John, do you love me more than these?"
>
> "Yes, Lord," he said, "you know that I love you."
>
> Jesus said, "Feed my lambs."
>
> Again Jesus said, "Simon son of John, do you love me?"
>
> He answered, "Yes, Lord, you know that I love you."
>
> Jesus said, "Take care of my sheep."
>
> The third time he said to him, "Simon son of John, do you love me?"
>
> Peter was hurt because Jesus asked him the third time, "Do you love me?" He said, "Lord, you know all things; you know that I love you."
>
> Jesus said, "Feed my sheep."
>
> —John 21:15–17

Jesus is teaching a truth here that John (standing nearby during this conversation) would write about in his first letter from exile in Patmos. John would come to understand what Peter was learning, something so central to the faith that the Holy Spirit prompted John to say it over and over throughout 1 John. Here it is.

> Dear friends, let us love one another, for love comes from God. Everyone who loves has been born of God and knows God. Whoever does not love does not know God, because God is love.... We love because he first loved us. If we say we love God yet hate a brother or sister, we are liars.

For if we do not love a fellow believer, whom we have seen, we cannot love God, whom we have not seen. And he has given us this command: Those who love God must also love one another.

—1 John 4:7–8, 19–21

In other words, loving God means loving people—and loving people means loving God. You cannot ever separate these two interdependent truths!

I hear people talk about how leaders are strategic, visionary, committed, strong, courageous, fearless, chosen by God, empowered for impact, and called to a great mission. All this is important. Yet there is an overriding practice every leader must turn into a lifestyle—love.

Don't miss the point: leaders are lovers!

4. Lead

Okay, this is obvious, I suppose. After all, leaders should ... lead!

I can tell you from experience that not everyone with the role of leader actually leads. Sounds crazy, but it's true. There are teachers who cannot teach, baseball players who cannot get a hit to save their lives, politicians who cannot govern, pastors who cannot preach, and leaders who cannot—or choose not to—lead! Leadership can be challenging.

Leadership requires commitment and sacrifice. "No one who puts his hand to the plow and looks back is fit for service in the kingdom of God" (Luke 9:62 NIV). Those were hard words about full devotion, spoken to an audience that did not understand the level of commitment Christ desires and the cost of following him. Leaders prove their love for Christ by their commitment to his followers (John 21:15–19).

It is easy to have group meetings; it is harder to make disciples. Small group leaders serve in a spirit of commitment, not convenience. It takes courage, resolve, and perseverance when you are disappointed or weary. Leaders need to remain committed to the cause, to Christ, to the church, and to the people in their group. Are you willing to do what it takes to effectively lead and care for your people?

Why leaders do not lead

Here are a few reasons why group leaders do not lead.

- They confuse mere facilitation with leadership.
- They fear that they will appear overbearing.
- They think people don't need another "leader" in their lives.
- They fear that they are viewed as a boss.

- They think leaders are control freaks, and they refuse to become one.
- They feel spiritually inferior to some or all group members.
- They do not know the Bible as well as others do.
- They are intimidated by hard questions and difficult people.
- They believe compromise and consensus always trump leadership.
- They don't feel "visionary" enough.
- They have failed in the past and have failed some members of the group.
- They are afraid to fail.
- The cost of leadership is sometimes too high.
- They feel lonely sometimes as a leader. Who needs that?

What can get in the way of your leadership? Do you have fears that keep you from exercising leadership when you know it's the right thing to do?

REFLECTION

Leadership Fears

Which of the perspectives in the preceding list cause you to hesitate as a leader? What other perspectives not on the list concern you?

I remember when ministry partner Russ Robinson and I were talking about leadership in challenging situations, and he made this statement: "We have to remember that if there is no resistance, there is no need for a leader."

It was kind of a "duh" moment for me, as well as an encouragement. It is going to be hard; I am going to doubt my abilities; I am going to experience fear and frustration with myself and others; there will be resistance—from within and without.

Self-leadership

That is why God calls people to take on the role and responsibilities of leaders. As a leader, you will need to excel in two areas—leading your group and leading yourself. Self-leadership is often the greater challenge. Here are some things to consider in order to lead yourself well, with truth and grace.

1. *Face reality about your sin and weakness.* Always the first job of a leader, naming reality about myself is of prime importance. I do not like this part. It means honest reflection, humble confession, and a commitment to let it go and move ahead.

2. *Declare your personal dignity.* Remind yourself that in the eyes of God you are gifted, called, blessed, loved, forgiven, protected, significant, and loved (did I say that already?). This is your true identity in your relationship with Christ. Declare this daily!

3. *Take responsibility for your own growth.* It is up to you and me to read the book, have the conversation with a mentor, reflect on the Bible, expose the mind to new ideas, network with fresh thinkers, and engage in serious debate and discussion. It's our job!

4. *Pursue a life of simplicity and focus.* Rid yourself of the things that tangle up your leadership—unnecessary meetings, committees, and teams; stuff that clamors for attention; people who are draining and never desire to change; the tendency to vary from your core mission. You must ruthlessly shed these distractions so that you can give maximum energy to "this one thing I do" in the moments when such focus is required.

What would you add to this list?

REFLECTION

Self-Leadership

Which of the four areas in the preceding list requires your immediate attention? What steps can you take to grow in this area? *(Consider these options: read about how others face the challenge, ask mentors for help, meet with fellow leaders to learn their strategies, consult with your coach or overseer in the ministry structure at church, pray for wisdom and courage, and develop a simple plan with accountability from others.)*

Burnout claims many well-intentioned leaders. Listen to Paul's counsel to young Timothy: "Watch your life and doctrine closely" (1 Tim. 4:16). We need sound doctrine and sound leaders—leaders who have energy to carry out the ministry. Good leaders pay close attention to themselves; they watch their lives. Are you emotionally, spiritually, and physically caring for yourself so that you have energy—capacity—to lead your group?

Never sacrifice your life and family on the altar of ministry. God does not want you frazzled and exhausted while you seek to serve others. There are seasons of hardship and difficulty, but you cannot sustain a fruitful ministry amid frequent exhaustion and constant pressure. Here are some tips to help sustain you and avoid burnout.

- *Set boundaries around your time and priorities.* Learn to say no regardless of the disappointment you might cause others.
- *Create margin in your life.* Plan some space into your schedule, three to four unscheduled blocks of time for fun, friends, rest, and responding to the inevitable crisis.
- *Be diligent to replenish your reserve.* Practice solitude and take time for celebration. Fill your tank with joy, rest, and extended community with God.

There will be more on personal practices later in this chapter.

Participate in a leadership community

If you do not already meet regularly with a group of other small group leaders and ministry staff, consider forming such a group. Ask your pastoral leaders to help. A leadership community will provide you with many resources for leading more effectively. In a thriving leadership community where you are among peers and more experienced leaders, you will be able to

share strategies;
tell stories about life change;
diagnose common problems and challenges;
learn creative ideas for discussions, prayer, and group events;
discover fresh ideas for Bible study;
support one another in prayer;
become a "board of directors" for decision making;
learn new leadership skills;
process mistakes or failures in the safety of doing so with people who have been there;

share resources with one another—books, CDs, online resources; remember what we covered earlier in this book: *No one leads alone.*

A leadership community will serve you and the church well. It will be a place to bring potential leaders and apprentice leaders who need fresh vision and encouragement for stepping up to leadership.

REFLECTION

Listen, Learn, Love, and Lead

Now that you have had some time to work through these four areas, identify one thing in each area to learn about or work on in the next thirty days as you lead your group. If you are not currently leading, think about the four areas with respect to your first meeting someday. What might serve you best as you prepare for leadership?

Listen

Learn

Love

Lead

PERSONAL SPIRITUAL PRACTICES FOR GROUP LEADERS

You have just completed a section designed to give you clarity in four leadership practices. Now let's look at the personal spiritual practices that will help you maintain your spiritual and emotional health as you lead others in a group.

Why Are Spiritual Practices So Important?

The apostle Paul compares the Christian life to running a marathon. We run to win, reaching forward to what lies ahead, always pressing on toward the goal for the prize of the upward call of God in Christ Jesus. The runner, like the Christian, has a goal, a strategy, and a finish line (1 Cor. 9:24–27; Phil. 3:12–14). A race takes stamina, diligence, preparation, and discipline. If we were runners, we would never try to enter a race without proper training. In training, we learn to pursue certain practices that will enable us to endure the race.

In 1 Corinthians 9:24–27 Paul says, "Do you not know that in a race all the runners run, but only one gets the prize? Run in such a way as to get the prize. Everyone who competes in the games goes into strict training. They do it to get a crown that will not last; but we do it to get a crown that will last forever. Therefore I do not run like a man running aimlessly; I do not fight like a man beating the air. No, I beat my body and make it my slave so that after I have preached to others, I myself will not be disqualified for the prize" (NIV).

Spiritual "disciplines," or practices, will help you live the Christian life with authenticity, stamina, and perseverance. You practice these disciplines in preparation for hearing God's voice. They prepare you for the race you were intended to run. Hebrews 5:8 says that Jesus "learned obedience from what he suffered." Practicing the disciplines prepares you to meet God and understand his will, to battle temptation, to engage in loving relationships, to make wise and godly decisions, to love your family, and to be a leader in your area of ministry. There is great joy in being disciplined enough to finish the race. Paul wrote at the end of his life, "I have fought the good fight, I have finished the race, I have kept the faith. Now there is in store for me the crown of righteousness, which the Lord, the righteous Judge, will award to me on that day — and not only to me, but also to all who have longed for his appearing" (2 Tim. 4:7–8). Like Paul, be a leader who finishes the race well.

What Are the Spiritual Disciplines?

Dallas Willard, in *The Spirit of the Disciplines*, and Richard Foster, in *Celebration of Discipline*, each have compiled a list of spiritual disciplines and practices that they believe Christ modeled. (You can refer to their books for a complete discussion.) Spiritual disciplines are typically organized into two categories: the disciplines of abstinence (or letting go) and the disciplines of engagement.

Disciplines of letting go

These practices allow us to relinquish something in order to gain something new. We abstain from busyness in ministry, family life, and work. We stop talking for a while to hear from God. We give up buying another material possession to experience God more fully. First Peter 2:11 warns us to "abstain from sinful desires, which war against your soul." Identify what is keeping you from experiencing greater strength and perspective. Do you talk too much? Are possessions controlling you? Are you too worried about what others think? Choose disciplines that will help you become more dependent on God.

Solitude: spending time alone to be with God. Find a quiet place to be alone with God for a period of time. Use the Bible as a source of companionship with God. Listen to him. Remain alone and still.

Silence: removing noisy distractions to hear from God. Find a quiet place away from noise to hear from God. Write your thoughts and impressions as God directs your heart. Silence can occur even in the midst of noise and distraction. But you must focus your attention on your soul. This could mean talking less or talking only when necessary. And it could mean turning off the radio and the TV.

Fasting: skipping a meal (or meals) to find greater nourishment from God. Choose a period of time to go without food. Drink water and, if necessary, take vitamin supplements. Feel the pain of having an empty stomach and depend on God to fill you with his grace.

Frugality: learning to live with less money and still meet basic needs. Before buying something new, choose to go without or pick a less expensive alternative that will serve your basic needs. Live a simple, focused life.

Chastity: choosing to abstain from sexual pleasures for a time (those pleasures that are deemed morally right in the bond of marriage) to find higher fulfillment in God. Decide together as a couple to set aside time to go without sexual pleasures in order to experience a deeper relationship with God in prayer.

Secrecy: serving God without self-promtion, so others are unaware of our service. Give in secret. Serve behind the scenes in a ministry that you are assured few will know about.

Sacrifice: giving overabundantly of our resources to remind us of our depen-
dence on Christ. Choose to give more of your time or finances to God
than you normally would.

Disciplines of engagement

Dallas Willard writes, "The disciplines of abstinence must be coun-
ter-balanced and supplemented by disciplines of engagement [activity]."
Choosing to participate in activities nurtures our souls and strengthens us
for the race ahead.

Study: spending time reading the Scriptures and meditating on their mean-
ing and importance in our lives. Scripture is our source of spiritual
strength. Choose a time and a place to feed from it regularly.

Worship: offering praise and adoration to God. His praise should continually be on our lips and in our thoughts. Read psalms, hymns, or spiritual songs, or sing to God daily using a praise tape. Keep praise ever
before you as you think of God's activity and presence in your life.

Service: choosing to be a humble servant, as Christ was to his disciples when he
washed their feet. Consider opportunities to serve in the church and in
the community. Learn to do acts of kindness that otherwise might be
overlooked (help someone do yard work, clean a house, buy grocer-
ies, run an errand, and so on).

Prayer: talking with God about your relationship with him and about the con-
cerns of others. Prayer involves both talking to God and listening to
him. Find time to pray without the distraction of people or things.
Combine your prayer time with meditation on the Scriptures in
order to focus on Christ.

Community: mutual caring and ministry in the body of Christ. Meet regularly with other Christians to find ways to minister to others.
Encourage one another.

Confession: regularly admitting your sins to the Lord and to other trusted
individuals. As often as you are aware of sin in your life, confess it to
the Lord and to those you may have offended.

Submission: humbling yourself before God and others while seeking account-
ability in relationships. Find faithful brothers or sisters in Christ who
can lovingly hold you accountable for your actions and for your
growth in Christ.

As you can see, that is a very large list. It can be overwhelming. These
practices are not meant for immediate consumption, like a fast-food dinner
on the way to a soccer game. They are exercises for the spiritual life, which

is a marathon, not a sprint. As you mature and as you move through the various seasons of life, you will face challenges and opportunities that will drive you toward certain disciplines. You will find yourself learning new practices along the way, especially as you connect with other believers and leaders who are using those exercises for personal growth.

Of the many spiritual disciplines listed above, I want to focus on just three for you to incorporate regularly into your life—alone and with your church community.

Practice 1: Study

Reading the Bible regularly is food for the hungry soul, knowledge for the searching mind, and encouragement for the fainting heart. I have learned various ways of reading and studying the Bible over the years, especially from other leaders and teachers in the church, both current and through the ages.

> *Study the Bible for yourself, but* not *just by yourself!* Yes, learn to study the Bible. Take online courses; wrestle with the text; do your own work. Spend time alone digging into the Word of God. But don't stop there! Talk with others, use commentaries and reference guides. Listen to teachers on the sections or topics you are studying. Your understanding of the text is important, but it could be prejudiced, narrow, or even wrong. Others in the body of Christ, especially those with teaching and scholarship gifts, can help you understand what you are reading.
>
> *Never engage the text without encountering the Author.* Too many people fall in love with the Bible and rarely find themselves in deep fellowship with the primary writer—God! When you read, expect to meet God. Expect to feel his presence and to hear his voice and to sense his life in you. Don't just let your mind be captured by the truth; let your heart be captivated by Jesus.
>
> *Read the Bible for transformation, not just information.* Read the Bible asking these questions: How shall I now live? What difference does knowing this make? Then pray: Holy Spirit, please place your finger on areas of life where I need to change and grow and turn toward God.

Three approaches to reading the Bible

These methods can be used as a group or alone. In this section, let's focus on your own Bible reading.

1. Read and reflect

There are four movements in this approach.

1. *Prepare your heart.* Sit quietly or listen to worship music or read a devotional thought to open your heart to God. If you need coffee, get it. If you need a quiet place, find it. Take time to be quiet before God, allowing the clutter and noise to subside in your head.

2. *Listen to the Word.* Read the text several times. Read it slowly, repeatedly, and with a heart that seeks to meet God.

3. *Meditate.* Take words, phrases, or truths that emerge from the text and chew on them. Think about them. Ponder their significance. Repeat them in your head or out loud. Consider memorizing some of it. Take time to reflect on the significance of these words. What is God saying to you, to his church, to our world?

4. *Respond.* Consider the action you must take. Sometimes it is simply to sit and enjoy God and his truth. Sometimes there is something to obey or someone you might need to meet with. The focus in this method is to simply commune with God and enjoy his presence. Trust the Word and the Spirit to speak.

2. Engage and examine

In this approach, read the text and engage with the deep and challenging phrases or truths in the passage. Here you will not simply meditate on it or think about it—you will study the passage more rigorously.

1. *Ask questions of the text.* What is it saying? What words are repeated or important? Who is the audience? Who is the author? What is the purpose of the book or section? What truths or promises are listed? What is the context? What is the setting and culture?

2. *Determine what it meant and what it means.* What did the author want the original audience to know? In light of their culture and setting and spiritual condition, what was the writer communicating? Try to discern what truths, principles, or commands also apply to our lives and culture today. You will likely need a study Bible, a Bible dictionary, a commentary on that book of the Bible, and other written or online resources. Ask your church leaders what they recommend for Bible study tools and resources.

3. *Search the Scriptures for similar texts or themes or ideas.* Use the concordance at the back of the Bible or in the margins for cross-references. Start with passages in the same book of the Bible, then from the

same author, then go to other references. Where else did the writers of Scripture talk about this truth, place, idea, or character?

4. *Summarize the learning or wrestle with the tension, the unknown.* Given the time you have, pause and try to summarize what you have learned from your study. Write down some conclusions or questions that you still have. How would you teach what you have learned to a ten-year-old? That is a good test.

3. Observe and obey

The focus on this approach is heavily on the "so what?" How shall we now *live*?

Be aware that each approach has challenges

Remember, no approach is flawless or will do full justice to all the richness of the Bible. You can spend weeks on a given passage and only scratch the surface. That is the beauty and wonder of the Bible. Though very simple and clear, enough for even a child to understand, it also holds deep truths and mysteries that take years to fully grasp, experience, and practice. The well never runs dry.

Here are some cautions for each method.

Read and reflect. You might be tempted to ignore challenging passages or avoid rigor required in the text, shying away from studying it later.

Engage and examine. This can become an intellectual exercise if learning content and gathering information become the focus.

Observe and obey. You might move too quickly to application without reflection, meeting the author, sitting with the truth you are reading.

Of course, you could take a text and use all three approaches in a given week. Generally, the passage of the Bible and your own growth needs will help you discern which approach is best for any given reading exercise. If you have only a few minutes, approach 1 or approach 3 might be best. If you are preparing for a lesson, approach 2 would be good, assuming you have at least an hour.

Practice 2: Prayer

A basic approach for prayer

Effective leaders have vital prayer lives. Here are some guidelines to help you become a more effective leader and person of prayer. We've found them to be useful and powerful principles.

First we'll give you an outline for praying, then some principles for prayer from Romans 8, and then some prerequisites for answered prayer.

An outline for prayer: ACTS

Adoration (Psalm 100)

1. Choose one of God's attributes; praise him for his character.
2. Paraphrase a psalm.
3. Pray back a psalm.

Confession (1 John 1:9). Take an inventory of yesterday. Is there anything there that displeases the Lord? Make a list, ask God for forgiveness, then destroy it.

Thanksgiving (Luke 17:11–19; 1 Thess. 5:16–18). List your blessings, using the following categories:

1. Spiritual
2. Relational
3. Material
4. Physical

Supplication (Phil. 4:6–7; 1 John 5:14–15). Categorize your needs under the following headings:

1. Major concerns
2. Relational
3. Physical or material
4. Spiritual
5. Character

Listen quietly—wait for the Spirit to lead and guide. (For more on this, see Bill Hybels's book *Too Busy Not to Pray.*)

Four principles of prayer: Rom. 8:26–29

Romans 8:26–29 gives us some insights into prayer. As you read the passage and meditate on it, you will find some of the principles listed below. God certainly answers prayer, but not always in the way we expect. This information will help you understand how God responds to prayer.

1. The Holy Spirit helps us to know what and how to pray (v. 26).
2. The Holy Spirit intercedes on our behalf (v. 26).
3. God hears our hearts more than the words in prayer (v. 27).
4. Prayer is always answered (vv. 28–29), though not always according

to our agenda. Bill Hybels has coached many people about God's four basic responses to our prayers:

No. Your request is not in God's will (2 Sam. 12:15–16, 22–23; Matt. 26:36–39).

Slow. Your request is not in God's will at this time (Gen. 15:2–6; 21:2; John 11:3, 6, 14–15, 17, 43–44).

Grow. Your motives are wrong (Num. 14:26–45; James 4:3).

Go. Your request, timing, and spiritual condition are okay. Yes! (1 Kings 18:36–39 [cf. James 5:17–18]; Acts 12:5–7, 12–17).

Prerequisites for answered prayer

Though it is clear from Scripture that God always answers our prayers in some manner (as we mentioned above), there are also some guidelines for effective praying. Certain practices or attitudes can hinder your prayers, and in such cases God will not respond to them. The following passages help us understand that we must be in a right relationship with God and with others in order for God to hear our prayers.

Harboring unconfessed sin will put a barrier between you and God (Ps. 66:18).

God hears the prayers of people who obey his commands (1 John 3:22–23).

God will not hear the prayers of people who have wrong or selfish motives (James 4:3).

We are instructed to pray according to God's will, not according to ours (1 John 5:14–15).

When we pray, we are to ask in faith. Unbelief is a barrier to answered prayer (Mark 11:22–24).

An ongoing abiding life in Christ (having regular fellowship with him) will allow your prayers to be heard. However, when fellowship is broken, so is communication with God (John 15:7).

Sometimes we don't have answered prayers because we do not ask. We are to pursue appropriate requests regularly and bring them to God (Luke 11:9).

Praying in the Spirit (that is, under the control of the Holy Spirit) is also a prerequisite. We must also persevere in our praying (Eph. 6:18).

If you do not forgive someone for wrongs that person has done to you, then God will not forgive you. Restored and right relationships are essential for open communication with God (Matt. 6:14–15; Mark 11:25).

We are to pray with thankful hearts. Those of us who come before God without a spirit of thankfulness will find that our prayers are not heard (Phil. 4:6).

Four guidelines for prayer
1. Pray to God about everything (Phil. 4:6–7).
2. Pray consistently (1 Thess. 5:17).
3. Pray according to the name of Jesus—that is, according to the will of Jesus (John 16:24).
4. Pray with bold confidence (Heb. 4:16).

The role of the Spirit

A common characteristic of great leaders in the Scriptures is that their lives and ministries were led by the Holy Spirit. In Ephesians 5:18–19 (NIV) Paul says, "Do not get drunk on wine, which leads to debauchery. Instead, be filled with the Spirit. Speak to one another with psalms, hymns and spiritual songs. Sing and make music in your heart to the Lord." A person who is intoxicated with wine lives irresponsibly before God and others. By contrast, a person who is filled with the Holy Spirit leads a responsible, Christ-honoring life characterized by authentic relationships with God and others.

How can you live a life in the Spirit? Or better said, how can you be continually led by the Holy Spirit? As a leader, you must allow the Holy Spirit to have his way in your life. This will empower your leadership and will result in your having the fruit of the Spirit.

Remember, according to Jesus in John 16:5–15, the Spirit is your helper, your guide, and your teacher of truth. Here are some ways to be sure that you are following in the way of the Holy Spirit.

Keep in step with the Spirit

Another way that the Bible says this is to keep in step with, or walk with, the Spirit. Keeping in step with the Spirit means allowing him to control you as you read Scripture, pray, and hear God's voice. When you submit your will to God's will, the Spirit can control more of your life and direct your path.

Set your mind on the things of the Spirit

Romans 8:6–9 (NIV) tells us, "The mind of sinful man is death, but the mind controlled by the Spirit is life and peace; the sinful mind is hostile to God. It does not submit to God's law, nor can it do so. Those controlled by the sinful nature cannot please God. You, however, are controlled not by the sinful nature but by the Spirit, if the Spirit of God lives in you. And if anyone does not have the Spirit of Christ, he does not belong to Christ." Since the Spirit of God already dwells in you, you simply need to yield yourself to him and allow him to take control of your life. Focusing on the things of the Spirit means paying attention to God-honoring relationships, decisions, conversations, thoughts, and activities.

Galatians 5 explains that a life lived in the Spirit, with obedience to Christ's commands, will yield the fruit of the Spirit—"love, joy, peace, patience, kindness, goodness, faithfulness, gentleness and self-control" (vv. 22–23). However, when we are not yielded to the Spirit, we either quench the Spirit (1 Thess. 5:19) by ignoring the Word of God or grieve the Spirit (Eph. 4:30) by bringing resentment and anger to relationships. Sin always pours water on the fire of the Holy Spirit.

By applying the principles we've just discussed, you can live a Spirit-filled life and allow God to work through you to be an effective leader. To learn more about the work of the Spirit in the life of a leader and in the life of other believers, read the following passages. It would be great to work through some of these as a small group to encourage others to live a life in the Spirit.

The baptism of the Holy Spirit (1 Cor. 12:13)
The indwelling ministry of the Holy Spirit (Rom. 8:11; 1 Cor. 3:16; 2 Tim. 1:14)
The filling ministry of the Holy Spirit (Acts 4:8; Acts 4:31; Eph. 5:18)
The convicting ministry of the Holy Spirit (John 16:7–11)
The regenerating ministry of the Holy Spirit (John 3:3–6; Titus 3:5–6)
The reassuring ministry of the Holy Spirit (1 Cor. 2:12–16; 1 John 4:13; 5:7–8)
The sanctifying ministry of the Holy Spirit (Rom. 8:11–12; 2 Cor. 3:18; 2 Thess. 2:13)
The teaching ministry of the Holy Spirit (John 16:13; 1 Cor. 2:13)
The intercessory ministry of the Holy Spirit (Rom. 8:26)
The empowering ministry of the Holy Spirit (Luke 4:14, 18–19; Acts 1:8; Rom. 15:13, 19)
The comforting ministry of the Holy Spirit (John 14:16)
The convicting work of the Holy Spirit (John 16:7)
The encouraging work of the Holy Spirit (Acts 9:31)
The believer's responsibility to be filled with the Holy Spirit (Gal. 5:16–26; Eph. 5:18)

Practice 3: Community

Relational integrity stems directly from authentic communal engagement. You are, at some level, the product of your community. Living with others, as Jean Vanier says, reveals our pride and ego, and yet it gives opportunities to be "for" others and share their lives. This practice keeps every leader from thinking too highly of himself or herself and from self-absorption.

You might be thinking, "I lead a small group, so I have community already." If the group you are leading provides you with a deeply connected, trust-filled, grace-based, safe environment in which you can be yourself and share your struggles, great! If not, you need to find a couple of people who understand you well. And even if your group is great (as many of mine have been through the years), there is often the need to enjoy some community life with other leaders who know the joys and heartaches of leadership.

Jesus connected more deeply with Peter, James, and John. Paul often had one or two close partners with him, doing ministry and sharing life (Titus, Luke, Timothy, Priscilla and Aquila). So what about you?

A band of brothers, a society of sisters

Every leader needs a relational support network. Your life in an authentic community will provide the care, the opportunities for personal growth, and the place to simply "be" that you need. When leaders fail to experience such a community—whether in the group they lead or with some other group leaders—they will eventually find their souls withering and their hearts becoming despondent.

For many leaders, this is usually a men's or women's group. But it can also be a mixed group. The key is what you find there. Here are some questions to ask about such a group for you, a leader seeking community.

1. Does the group treat me as a leader in a role or as a person in relationship? (You want the latter.)
2. Is this a place where I find safety and friendship?
3. Does the community offer accountability that is not judgmental but rather inspirational, where we come alongside one another to help each other stay the course and work through sin or brokenness?
4. Can I share frustrations about ministry challenges without fear that others in the group will become discouraged with the church?
5. Are there one or two others in the group who could be close spiritual friends with whom I share deeply and confess the deeper personal needs and faults I have?

6. Is there a culture of grace and truth which, over time, will allow me to walk more closely with Christ and others?
7. Do others in the group understand the specific needs, disappointments, and frustrations that accompany leadership in a spiritual setting?

Working through these questions will help you and potential members of the group create the environment necessary for real community.

REFLECTION

My Personal Community

Take a few moments to think and pray about who might be in your inner circle of fellow leaders, people with whom you can share life and speak the truth in love.

No one leads alone

"No one stands alone!" is a mantra I have championed for years. Group life matters. We want a place in community for everyone. But we should add, "No one leads alone!" Authentic leadership requires a leader to rely on others, empower others, and learn from others.

In addition to having a place in community for yourself, here are some insights about authentic, communal leadership that will prevent you from becoming a lone ranger leader.

Authentic leaders allow others to "outperform" them. "God save us from *becoming* know-it-all leaders," said Dave Fleming. Such leaders have the "solo shepherd" syndrome and cripple the body instead of allowing each part to do its work (see Eph. 4:15 – 16). In groups, we draw out the giftedness and experience of others, releasing them into ministry. Everyone in the circle has something to offer. Sadly, some leaders fear that members will outperform them. But this never worried Jesus—in fact, it was his desire. His follwers will do "even greater things than these," he said in John 14:12. The best leaders empower others to outperform them and can celebrate when that happens.

Authentic leaders align the group's vision with the church's mission. Almost as bad as know-it-all leaders are leave-me-alone leaders. Some small group leaders want no coaching or accountability. But group leaders must understand that their role is delegated to them by the people with spiritual authority in the church who, in turn, must give an account to Christ for the condition of the flock. Small groups exist to mobilize members *to carry out the ministry of the local church*. It is essential that your group aligns its specific purpose (Bible study, personal growth, recovery, and so on) with the overall mission of the church.

Authentic leaders learn from failure. Watch out for the I-can-fix-it-alone leader. In ministry, failure is fatal when a leader will not process it with others. Instead, a leader should name the failure and take steps to process the experience with others, building hope for future ministry success. For example, a group leader in student ministry takes the members of his group to a homeless shelter without informing parents. You can say to parents later, "I allowed my passion for giving students a look at the plight of the homeless to exceed my discernment in communicating to you. Please forgive me." Own your mistake and design a process that will build trust as you go forward with your group.

Don't be tempted to destroy the power of community by being alone or by leading alone. It's dangerous for you, and a deadly example for your small group to follow.

REFLECTION

My Leadership

As I think of my leadership role, how will I plan to become a communal leader so that I never lead alone and so that I have a group to help me along the way?

ADDITIONAL RESOURCES

On Leadership

Warren Bennis and Burt Nanus, *Leaders* (Harper and Row). Bennis and Nanus focus on managing yourself, creating vision, communicating your vision, developing trust, and organizational management. It is a book that emphasizes strategies for personal and organizational leadership.

Robert Clinton, *The Making of a Leader* (NavPress). Probably the best book on Christian leadership and the role of the Spirit. Clinton emphasizes the six stages of leadership development, and he establishes checkpoints to clarify where you are in each stage of the process. Also very helpful for maturing new leaders under your care.

Roberta Hestenes, *Using the Bible in Groups* (Westminster). A classic on how to do group Bible study and discussion.

J. Oswald Sanders, *Spiritual Leadership* (Moody). Sanders writes that spiritual leadership is the blending of natural and spiritual qualities. His book is a Christian classic. Though a little dated and written primarily to men, it is a thorough, biblically principled book on Christian leadership.

On Prayer

E. M. Bounds, *Power through Prayer* (Moody).
Richard Foster, *Prayer* (HarperSanFrancisco).
Bill Hybels, *Too Busy Not to Pray* (InterVarsity).

On the Holy Spirit

J. I. Packer, *Keep in Step with the Spirit* (Revell).
Charles Swindoll, *Flying Closer to the Flame* (Word).

On Evangelism

Scott Boren, *Missional Small Groups* (Baker).
Bill Hybels and Mark Mittelberg, *Becoming a Contagious Christian* (Zondervan).
Rebecca Pippert, *Out of the Saltshaker* (InterVarsity).
Lee Strobel, *The Case for Christ* (Zondervan).

On Spiritual Disciplines

Richard Foster, *Celebration of Discipline* (HarperSanFrancisco).
John Ortberg, *The Life You've Always Wanted* (Zondervan).
Dallas Willard, *The Spirit of the Disciplines* (HarperSanFrancisco).

Chapter 3

DEVELOPING YOUR APPRENTICE

SHARED LEADERSHIP

Now that you have a clear picture of your role as a group leader, it is time to build your leadership team. In order to assure that nobody stands alone in your church, you will need more groups, and that means more leaders. You were given a leadership baton, and the time will come for you to pass it to another. You will teach leadership lessons to your apprentice through practical on-the-job experiences in the small group.

Mutual leadership is a biblical pattern and a practical necessity. In this chapter, you will discover how to identify and develop your apprentice(s), giving him or her the skills and experiences needed to move forward. You will learn to delegate responsibilities to the person you are developing. Remember, no one leads alone!

You will see the fruit of your labor as you watch new leaders emerge from your group to guide others in the church toward spiritual growth. By developing apprentice leaders, you build a transformational community through your church.

Why Do I Need an Apprentice Leader?

The vitality and effectiveness of any local church is directly related to the quality of its leadership. The ministry of group life flourishes when churches emphasize the ongoing development of leaders in the body. It is the church's responsibility to identify and develop new leaders in order to accomplish the mission of the gospel and shepherd people. Jesus modeled this with the twelve disciples, and Paul exhorted Timothy to model this too (2 Tim. 2:2).

I am a firm believer in mobilizing and building up the body of Christ so that each member can accomplish the ministry God has given him or her, as described in Ephesians 4:12. It is the duty and privilege of all small group leaders to train up a new generation of leaders and to pass the baton effectively. The future hangs in the balance. Work together as a team—leaders, coaches, ministry builders—to continue to raise up new leaders for service in the kingdom.

REFLECTION

Your Leadership Legacy

Read quickly through Romans 16:1–16. There are lots of hard names to pronounce, but what else do you observe? What does this tell you about Paul and his approach to ministry?

What might your list look like someday? How many leaders will you leave in your wake?

What's the Difference between an Apprentice and an Assistant?

Remember, treat your apprentice as one who will lead and not as a person to whom you delegate unwanted details, projects, and "administrivia."

An Apprentice	An Assistant
Will be a leader someday	Will always support another leader
Shares responsibilities	Avoids responsibility
Engages in the same ministry as the leader	Does what the leader *does not* want to do
Helps lead the meeting	Only helps prepare for the meeting
Focuses on leadership skills	Focuses on logistics
Has their eyes on the vision	Has their head in the details

You and your apprentice are partners in ministry, and the relationship should reflect that as you prepare for meetings, lead meetings, and share responsibilities between meetings.

How Do I Find Potential Apprentices?

1. Look for group members who take the group seriously.
2. Consider people who challenge your leadership. These people may be potential leaders who are frustrated because they have no opportunity to lead.
3. Look for gifted people whom you can recognize and affirm.
4. Pray regularly for new apprentices (Luke 6:12 – 16).
5. Look for people who embrace the small group vision.
6. Observe people in your ministry as they perform tasks or work with people. Give them additional ministry opportunities and responsibilities to see if perhaps they have some leadership potential.
7. Try to look for people who exhibit the following spiritual, emotional, and social qualifications:

   • Spiritual qualifications

     Is it evident God is working in their life?
     Are they self-feeders? (Do they consistently nurture their own spiritual growth through time in God's Word and in prayer?)
     Are they eager to learn? (Do they actively participate in spiritual discussions?)
     Do they share the vision of small groups?

   • Emotional qualifications

     Are they secure enough to be vulnerable and honest with the group?

Are they emotionally stable? (Are they aware of their own strengths and weaknesses and not subject to mood swings that affect the group dynamic?)

How do they respond to confrontation about their need for character growth? Defensively? Humbly?

- Social qualifications

Do they openly participate without dominating this discussion?

Are they able to listen to others in a caring way?

Are they able to facilitate discussion?

REFLECTION

Identifying an Apprentice

List the names of potential leaders. Think about group members, friends, people taking the same classes with you at church, ministry team participants, new believers who have leadership backgrounds in education or business, coworkers, teammates in sports, and so on.

1.

2.

3.

4.

5.

How Do I Overcome the Typical Objections from Potential Leaders?

1. *"I just don't have the time."* People make time for things they consider important. Share the importance of apprentice leadership in the body of Christ. Cast a vision for the life change that can occur as they participate in this new role as an apprentice.

2. *"I don't have the gift of leadership."* Encourage people by reminding them that leadership is mostly character. It takes time to develop character and competence. If you believe someone has the basic character qualities of a potential leader, assure them that you will make sure they get the appropriate training so they have the skills they need to be effective.

3. *"I'm not the leadership type."* Explore what the person means by "leadership type." They may have a definition of leadership that is not biblical. They may view a leader as someone who is in charge and in control, as opposed to someone who can facilitate life change by caring for, discipling, and loving others.

How Do I Confirm That I Have the Right Person as a Potential Apprentice?

1. Make sure they meet your ministry leaders at the church.
2. Check with others who have ministered with them or who know them.
3. Confirm that they have a teachable spirit and are willing to learn.

What If I Have Trouble Finding an Apprentice?

Recruiting apprentice leaders is a spiritual battle. The Evil One is not pleased when we develop new leaders who can impact the body of Christ and reach the world for Christ. Though coaches and other ministry leaders, functioning as quality control managers, will help in choosing your apprentice, the role of the Holy Spirit and prayer are essential. Apprentice formation is as important as evangelism, because an apprentice will go on someday to create group life and ultimately reach more people.

What Information Does a Potential Apprentice Need?

1. Describe the role of a group leader. Assure the potential apprentice that he or she is not expected to fulfill the job description requirements to the same degree that a leader would. Remember, the role he or she is considering is that of a developing (apprentice) leader.
2. Provide a clear picture of the time frame for apprentice development. An apprentice requires approximately twelve to eighteen months of development before leading a small group on his or her own. This varies depending on the needs of a given ministry and the maturity of the apprentice.
3. Explain that adequate training and resources are available for an apprentice's growth and encouragement.
4. Communicate the vision and values of the small group ministry. The apprentice should attend the required training events of the church. If the person is not yet affirmed as a participating member in the church, work with church leaders to help him or her enter the process (if your church has a formal membership requirement for leaders).

REFLECTION

What Concerns Do I Have about Developing an Apprentice?

It is sometimes difficult to find an apprentice, someone who is willing to step up into a leadership development role. Perhaps you need to look for *people* instead of *leaders* when considering potential apprentices. We leaders — especially if we've been at it awhile — tend to look at others through the lenses of our own gifts, abilities, and experiences as leaders. So we quickly disqualify people.

Read through the following thoughts and questions and see if they provoke some fresh thinking and strategies on your part.

1. Recall your first real leadership role — at work, church, home, or school — and try to remember what that felt like. Perhaps it was scary or overwhelming. Did you succeed? Fail? Learn a lot along the way?
2. Did someone take a risk by putting you in leadership? Did you have the freedom to fail?
3. Have you lost your boldness? You stepped up to lead a group. That took some courage and was a bit risky — for you, the church, and the group! So be courageous again and make the ask!
4. What is keeping you from making a bold ask, inviting someone to share leadership with you and to move toward their own leadership role someday?
5. Perhaps you need help from your church staff or your ministry leader. Don't be afraid to ask. They will pray with you and help you create a strategy for finding and developing a future leader.

I Need to Develop an Apprentice Leader — Any Tips?

1. Work through this book with your apprentice. Select various sections and discuss how the two of you can apply the principles and information to your group.
2. Continue to model group leadership to your apprentice. Your example is probably the only example of small group leadership that your apprentice has ever seen.
3. Allow your apprentice to lead. Continue to delegate areas of responsibility to him or her.
4. Make sure that you and your apprentice are regularly giving feedback to one another. When your apprentice leads a portion of the meeting, provide him or her with feedback, and vice versa. Create a list of questions with which, or areas on which, to evaluate one another.

5. Pray regularly with your apprentice for his or her personal needs and leadership development.

6. Help your apprentice determine what types of skill training would best fit in his or her stage of development. Work with your coach to direct your apprentice to the right classes or training opportunities.

7. Bring your apprentice with you whenever you are involved in ministry. If you are going to visit someone who is sick, bring your apprentice. If you are planning to attend a ministry meeting, make sure your apprentice comes with you. Remember to involve your apprentice in meetings with your coach or staff leadership at the church.

8. Help your apprentice find a ministry partner and future apprentice. You can never have too many apprentices. In order to develop new groups and leaders, you will need to identify new apprentice leaders.

9. Consider using the Apprenticeship Planner that follows. This will help you think through how you will work with your apprentice each month. The planner is divided into four sections: (1) the apprentice's involvement in meetings, (2) the apprentice's work with members, (3) the apprentice's personal development, and (4) long-term planning and goals. Sit down each month with your apprentice and work through the planner together.

10. Walk your apprentice through the process of becoming a participating member of the church, if that is required.

MATERIAL TO USE WHEN WORKING WITH YOUR APPRENTICE LEADER

When you find and begin meeting with an apprentice, the following material will be helpful for the person to read and work through with you. Since your apprentice is going to be a leader someday, make sure he or she has a copy of *Leading Life-Changing Small Groups*.

If I Become an Apprentice, What Can I Expect?

The journey from apprentice to leader is an exciting and challenging experience. In the apprentice development process, you will need to pay attention to certain rules of the road, rights of passage, and responsibilities given to you.

Rules of the road (qualifications)

Small group leadership is essentially the combination of character and skills.

Character	Skills
Must be developed	Can be provided
Takes time	Take practice and time
Can disqualify you from leadership	Can delay you from leadership
Involves your relationship to God and others	Involves your performance of a task
Is an inward measure	Are outward measures
Is tested in adversity but developed in quiet times	Are practiced in quiet times but tested in adversity

Biblical guidelines for character and skills

Baseline Character	Baseline Skills
Mark 10:35–45 (serve)	1 Tim. 3:1–7 (able to teach and manage responsibilities)
John 13:34–35 (love)	Titus 1:9 (able to stand up for sound doctrine)
1 Tim. 3:1–7 (integrity)	Rom. 12:8 (lead with diligence)
Gal. 5:22–23 (fruit bearing)	1 Peter 5:1–4 (shepherd with eagerness)

You are not expected to have developed all of these character traits by the time you become a small group leader. However, make it your aim to develop them as you mature in Christ.

The rites of passage (stages of apprentice development)

The three stages of apprentice development mirror the stages of early life. We've called the steps *dependence*, *independence*, and *interdependence*, and they mirror the stages of infancy, adolescence, and adulthood. As an apprentice, you may experience it this way:

1. *Dependence (infancy)*
   You explore leadership.
   You learn all you can.
   You become an observer.
   You rely on the leader.
   You develop a servant's heart.
   You exhibit strong dependence on the group.

2. Independence (adolescence)

You feel you can lead better than the leader can (*and that might be true at times*).

You think you don't need the group (*a bad assumption*).

You think you don't need support from the group leader anymore (*wrong*).

You are learning the leader's role.

Caution: Though this is a normal stage in development, it is also the most dangerous, for this is the time when you think that you are better than your leader and that you can easily lead the group. This feeling should be an indication that you're ready to take more responsibility for the group and share more directly in the leadership of it. Your goal is not to stay in this stage of independence. In Christ, we are to become dependent on one another. You must seek to move toward the third stage—interdependence.

3. Interdependence (adulthood)

You have earned the respect of the group.

You respect the group.

You need the group to affirm your leadership.

The group needs you.

You work with your leader as a team.

You share ownership with your leader.

You have combined the servant's heart with the leader's role.

Note: At this time, you may be preparing to lead your own group. Don't be surprised if feelings of ambivalence, uncertainty, fear, and inadequacy arise. This is normal and healthy. As a matter of fact, these feelings will give you the humility you need to become a leader. That they come is an indication to you that you are ready to launch out and lead, ready to be challenged further in your spiritual growth.

The Four Practices of an Apprentice Leader

Apprentices: These are the same four leadership practices as for a small group leader, but with a different focus as you develop your leadership abilities.

1. *Listen.* Listen to what the group leader is saying, how he or she is saying it, how he or she guides the discussion and responds to members. Practice your own listening skills as you hear people talking. What are they really saying with their facial expressions, posture, tone of

voice, and choice of words? Listen to the words, but listen beyond the words. Debrief with the group leader to see if you both had the same experience.

2. *Learn.* Learn from what your leader does and from what your leader does not do. Talk with your leader and debrief each meeting, discussing the pros and cons of the process. At this point, leadership is both caught and taught. Take advantage of skill training as it is offered or recommended.

3. *Love.* Love and support your leader and your group, doing all you can to be an example of the love of Christ toward group members. Take an active role in loving and caring for them. Work with your leader to share the care load in the group. There are people you can call, pray for (and with), and listen to.

4. *Lead.* Ask your leader to give you experience leading the group in various ways. Begin by leading the prayer time or facilitating the dialogue for one or two discussion questions. Over time, take more ownership and leadership in the group. You become a better leader by practicing leadership skills in a live setting. Now is the best time to do that. You should be leading six to eighteen months after you become an apprentice, depending on your experience and background before entering this role. Take advantage of this time to grow and master a variety of skills.

As you lead, begin to look for your own potential apprentices! Throughout your ministry as an apprentice, you ought to be looking for an apprentice as well. Ask yourself questions like these:

- Who might have leadership potential?
- Who has a servant's heart?
- Who is willing to learn?
- Do I have friends who are not participating in group life at the church?

Apprentice Development Worksheet

Consider using the following Apprenticeship Planner to work through together, leader and apprentice. Lay out a strategy for meetings, for content you will cover, for how you will work with group members, and so on. It's not complicated, but it requires some intentionality on your part.

APPRENTICESHIP PLANNER

Month	Meetings	Members	Personal Development	Long-Term Planning

ADDITIONAL RESOURCES

J. Robert Clinton and Paul D. Stanley, *Connecting* (NavPress, 1992). This book focuses on various kinds of mentoring relationships and how to develop them.

Bill Donahue and Greg Bowman, *Coaching Life-Changing Small Group Leaders* (Zondervan, 2012). Presents a framework for coaching small group leaders in a way that provides care, support, and leadership development.

Bill George, *True North* (Jossey-Bass, 2007). This resource and the workbook that goes with it are great tools for developing leaders at every level and include exercises for leaders to work through.

John Maxwell, *Developing the Leaders around You* (Nelson, 1995). Maxwell gives very practical guidelines and strategies for investing in and equipping the potential leaders you are working with.

Chapter 4

PURSUING SPIRITUAL GROWTH

NOT-SO-GREAT EXPECTATIONS

People have various expectations and ideas when it comes to group success. Everyone has their own way of defining what the optimal group is like. Each person comes with a list—sometimes in their subconscious—of what the group should be and do.

Your responsibility as a leader is to engage the group in a process of describing group health and coming to some consensus about how to achieve it together.

You might be asking, "What kind of atmosphere or culture must exist in a group or any small community of people so that they can work together, respect one another, grow personally, and accomplish the mission to which they feel called?"

We begin by talking about that environment—spiritual greenhouses—and then address the process that encourages transformation, the values that shape a group, and the structures that will help produce growth. You'll learn (1) how to create and cast a vision for your group, (2) the major components of group growth, (3) communication patterns, (4) the life stages through which the group will pass, and (5) how to design a covenant or ground rules that describe your commitment to one another.

BUILDING SPIRITUAL GREENHOUSES

Picture a greenhouse, a place where plants are nurtured toward growth and protected from harsh elements. Nurturing people in a group setting is similar because both plants and humans are organisms that respond to their environment as they grow.

Effective greenhouses have three basic characteristics. First, there is a *process* for growing plants. It involves planting in rich soil, watering regularly, applying nutritious fertilizer, and pruning away bad growth or removing weeds.

Second, there is a *structure* to protect the growth process from destructive forces. Wind, excess heat, heavy rains, extreme cold, and interaction with people or animals can create erosion, limit growth, or even cause death. Usually the structure is not attractive, and neither is it the focal point. Yet it is essential. Primarily made of glass, plastic, and metal, the structure protects the environment from destructive outside forces.

Third, there is the *growth* of the plants. Growth is expected in the greenhouse, and maturity is essential if plants are to one day be removed into other, less sheltered environments for which they were intended.

Process, structure, and growth. The first two are necessary if the third is to take place. Even with the right process and structure, some plants never reach their potential. They may barely grow or wither and die. We do not control the mysterious nature of the plant itself. The plant may have a disease or have a faulty internal structure or be unreceptive to the nutrients provided. We usually do not know why.

What Could Your Group Become?

Your group is a greenhouse, not a factory. The inputs do not guarantee the outputs. Paul made this point when writing a letter to the church in Corinth. "I planted the seed, Apollos watered it, but God has been making it grow" (1 Cor. 3:6).

"We worked the process within the structure of our ministry framework and design," Paul could have said, "but the mysteries of growth lie within each person as God works in them."

We do our best, with God's help, to create environments conducive to growth.

In the spiritual greenhouse of a small group exist the same three components found in a botanical greenhouse: process, structure, and growth. When a real greenhouse is effective, the result is not just the growth of individual plants and flowers but also beautiful landscapes, gardens, and parks.

You don't begin with a vision for a greenhouse. You have a vision for a world filled with beautiful landscapes, parks, and gardens. You build greenhouses with process, structure, and growth because you want to serve a greater, more majestic purpose—beauty.

The spiritual greenhouse we call a small group is similar. It's not our vision to have a small group. It's our vision to see Christ build his church, populated with people who love him, love his creation, love each other, and love people who don't yet know his love and grace. We envision a world filled with justice, hope, redemption, care, joy, love, and beauty. We launch small groups as environments to nurture the growth of people who will enter that world we long to create, with God's help and power.

Your group needs a vision for what it can be to change the world!

Let's start with the vision. Then we will move to process, structure, and growth within the group.

REFLECTION

The Future and Your Group

What will your group look like in a year? How will it be different? What do you hope you will become as you work within the spiritual greenhouse of group life, asking God to bring maturity and growth? How might the world be different because of your group?

Creating and Casting a Vision for Your Group

A vision is inspiring. It's a picture of a preferred future — what you want to become. A vision should be compelling and something around which your group can rally. For example, a group's vision statement might be something like this: "To become a Christlike community that is growing spiritually in the Word, relationally through mutual service, emotionally through honest communication, and numerically by adding new people to our group."

A vision must be:

1. *Concise.* It takes work to get a vision that can be stated in a sentence or two. This forces a group to choose very specific words to define the vision. Long, drawn out vision statements are hard to remember and difficult to communicate.
2. *Clear.* Make sure your vision has clarity and is easily understood. For example, in the vision statement above, it's clear that the group wants to grow personally and in numbers as a group.

3. *Consistent.* Is the vision consistent with the overall mission of the church? Your group's vision statement should relate directly to the purpose of the church.
4. *Compelling.* Is your vision statement something you can sink your teeth into? Is it something worth rallying around? Does it reflect the passion of the group?
5. *Collaborative.* Was the vision statement developed in collaboration with the group? Work with your group members (or at least the regular attendees) to develop a vision statement that reflects the values of the group as a whole. The more that people own the vision, the more they will make a commitment to it. Without a vision, your group will wander aimlessly and sense a lack of purpose.

REFLECTION

Group Vision

What do you and your group want to become? What kind of group will you need to be as you accomplish your purpose? Take time, perhaps a few minutes each meeting for two or three meetings, to shape your vision.

Our vision:

THE THREE ESSENTIALS FOR CREATING SPIRITUAL GREENHOUSES

1. The Process: Living Our Group Values

All groups operate according to certain values and expectations. Often these go unspoken or unwritten. In order to foster open communication and clarity about the purpose and values of the group, get your core values in writing. What follows are key values for small group relationships. This is only a sample set of values. You and your group should create your own list with the kinds of values central to your group. Again, consider your ministry when deciding on the right approach for your group. The important thing is that your members are committed to growing in interpersonal relationships and maturity in Christ.

Here are some examples of values.

1. *Affirmation.* It is important to create an atmosphere in which group members affirm and encourage one another, build each other up in Christ, and help each other grow.
2. *Availability.* Group members should be available to each other, and each member should be willing to make his or her resources available to the other members. People must make their time, attention, and insight, as well as material resources, available to each other in order to meet needs and serve one another.
3. *Prayer.* Prayer is valued in group life. The group comes together before God to praise, ask, confess, and thank him for all he has done. Prayer encourages group members to be humble, knowing that all comes from God. In prayer, they also feel valued and come to understand their own worth. As you see God move to answer your members' prayer concerns, the whole group will be encouraged.
4. *Openness.* Openness in the relationships within the group promotes honesty and an ease of sharing feelings, struggles, joys, and hurts. Reaching the goal of authentic relationships begins with being open with each other and with opening the group to new members.
5. *Honesty.* The desire to be honest with each other is critical to authentic relationships. In order to build trust in the group, members must speak the truth in love, so that "we will in all things grow up into him who is the head, that is, Christ" (Eph. 4:15).
6. *Safety.* Honest, open relationships must be safeguarded with an agreement that what is said in the group will remain confidential, that opinions will be respected, and that differences will be allowed.
7. *Confidentiality.* As part of the value of safety, confidentiality promotes openness by promising that whatever is shared within the confines of the group will not be repeated elsewhere.
8. *Sensitivity.* A commitment to being sensitive to the needs, feelings, backgrounds, and current situations of all members will help build relationships in the group.
9. *Accountability.* In authentic relationships, accountability is voluntary submission to another member (or other members) for support, encouragement, and help in a particular area of your life, giving them some responsibility for assisting you in that area.
10. *Evangelism.* As considered from a group perspective, evangelism is being committed to expanding the community of believers through such things as sharing the gospel with others, using the "open chair"

to inspire members to invite people into the group, or other types of outreach.

11. *Multiplication.* Having your group grow and eventually birth a new group enables the group to carry out the vision of seeing more people connected in Christian community, growing in their relationship with Christ.

12. *Care.* Showing care to one another and to other people is an expression of Christ's love. A caring group is often a safe group for new people. Care and compassion are essential for group life.

13. *Help.* Meeting practical needs by sharing gifts and abilities is a way to support one another. Helping each other with doing taxes, moving furniture, babysitting, making meals, doing homework, doing yard work, repairing cars, meeting financial challenges, and so on communicates that you care about all needs, not just crises or illnesses.

14. *Authenticity.* Being real with one another will open the group to greater truthfulness in discussions and create an environment of respect. It promotes humility and safety.

Choose four to six of these or create your own. You might want all of these in your group, but this list is too long, so try to develop four to six core values. You did some work on this in chapter 2, so now you can process this further on your own and then with your group.

REFLECTION

Crafting Your Values

1. Ask each member to list (or choose from a list like the one provided) the three values that matter most in order for the group to function well. Remember, these are values, which describe the relational environment you want for the group.
2. Gather all the lists and see what four to six values are most common or most essential.
3. Define each value in two or three sentences. You can assign this to groups of two, asking each pair to take one value, define it, and then share it with the entire group for revisions and input.
4. Create a final list of four to six core values with brief definitions that all members have at least 80 percent agreement with (every definition will never fully satisfy every member; you're looking for a general thumbs-up, not perfection).

continued on next page

Your list:

-
-
-
-
-
-

2. The Structure: Ground Rules and Covenants

Covenants are expressions of group values, expectations, or behaviors for which we hold ourselves mutually accountable. Covenants are agreements that create trust and build community. We enter into these relationships based on commitment and mutual acceptance. Ground rules or covenants are based on love and loyalty and are valid only if all members seek to fulfill the commitments and live by the values. In some cases, one party in a relationship may choose to keep a covenant despite the unfaithfulness of the other party (as God often did with Israel).

Not all groups have a written covenant or set of ground rules, but all groups have unwritten values or expectations that are understood by their members. When you develop a written covenant or set of ground rules, you are using the discipline of writing something on paper, which will bring more clarity and unity than simply discussing these things.

Keys to forming covenants or ground rules

1. The values must be generated by the group, not imposed by the leader.
2. The affirmations should always be in the form of "we" statements and must be affirmed by each individual.
3. Revisit the covenant on a periodic basis so that members remember their commitment to one another.
4. Remember to include both logistics and values that support group goals and purposes. For example, here is a very brief list.

Logistics
- Where and when we will meet
- How often we will meet

- Who is responsible for leading
- Who will handle meals or snacks
- Attendance expectations

Values
- Inviting new members
- Accountability
- Openness
- Confidentiality
- Acceptance

5. Covenants or ground rules must be formed over time, through a process that involves everyone.

Check with your ministry leadership about this process. They may already have a tool or some specific values they want every group to embrace. The following material is a guide for engaging in a healthy process together.

Creating ground rules or a covenant with your group

Meeting 1. Hand out a three-by-five-inch card and ask group members to write two or three values for the group. Define and rank these for your list. Talk about some basic commitments you want to make (when we meet, how often, and so on).

Meeting 2. Clarify your mission and try to create a clear statement of why you are meeting, at least for the next six months.

Meeting 3. Clarify your vision. What kind of people do you want to become as you live out your values and complete the mission? You might want to break into subgroups for some of this process, especially if there are more than six people in the group.

Meeting 4. Create a working document with all of this information on one page. This is not a contract but rather a statement of unity and commitment. Putting it in writing is a process for clarity. It is not something that cannot be revised or reshaped as you move ahead. Get it out and look at it every six months or so just to see if you still affirm this or want to change some things. It is a benchmark for progress, not laws to be obeyed.

Note: A sample covenant appears on page 95, but please create your own unique framework for your group.

SAMPLE COVENANT OR GROUND RULES

Leader_____ Apprentice(s) _____

1. The mission of our group is to:

   _____

   _____

   _____

2. We will meet for _____ weeks, after which we will evaluate our direction.
3. We will gather from _____ to _____ on _____ (day of the week), and we will arrive on time so we can start and end on time.
4. We will gather at _____ (place).
5. We will connect with Christ and one another by . . .
6. We will develop and grow by . . .
7. We will serve the church and the world by . . .

OUR VISION IS

To become a force for hope and change through love, service, and sacrificial living so we can encourage one another, and to impact our friends and neighbors for Christ.

OUR VALUES ARE

Participation. Everyone is given the right to their own opinion, and "dumb questions" are encouraged and respected.

Confidentiality. Anything of a personal nature that is said in the meeting is never repeated outside the meeting.

Authenticity. We will strive to be open and real with one another, respecting opinions and inviting people to share their lives and ideas. We will not judge people but will engage ideas and opinions truthfully.

Inclusivity. The group stays open to new people who can share our mission and values. The process for connecting with new people and inviting them to our group will be . . .

Group growth. We will seek to add members and develop leaders as God enables, and we will seek to give life to a new group in which others can experience the community we are enjoying by . . .

SHARED RESPONSIBILITIES

We will seek to share some or all of the following responsibilities: leader, host or hostess, prayer coordinator, event planner, administrator, social media, service project coordinator, and so on.

_____/_____

_____/_____

_____/_____

_____/_____

_____/_____

3. The Strategy for Growth: Essential Ingredients

Essential ingredients for growth in group life

All groups share some common objectives for growth. In *Walking the Small Group Tightrope*, Russ Robinson and I named six goals or objectives for a small group, recognizing that leaders pursue those six goals as they navigate a number of tensions along the way. Thus the tightrope image of holding something in tension so that the result is balance. For example, number 1 below recognizes a truth-life tension. A group can put all the weight toward knowing truth or toward sharing life. Both are good and both are essential in a group. To pursue spiritual growth, one must hold truth and life together in a kind of tension, moving back and forth between them to create harmony and balance.

Whether you are leading a task group, a children's group, a home group for adults, or a support group, these six components frame the context for your small group experience. A group may emphasize some of these components more than others, depending on the group's focus. All six should be present in the life of most small groups.

1. *Pursue spiritual transformation.* When the truth of Scripture meets the lives of group members, the opportunity for transformation exists. Some groups focus only on doctrinal truth and Bible study, while others primarily share needs and concerns. Groups seeking to be transformed into the image of Christ must read, study, and speak the truth and apply it to life. Such groups ask, "How will we change or respond to the truth that has been studied and discussed?" Don't settle for gaining information; pursue transformation. Allow the Holy Spirit to work the truth into your heart to produce lasting change and growth.

2. *Practice intentional development.* "Do we concentrate on caregiving or discipleship?" The answer is, "Both!" Groups in which members help one another grow while also providing care for people in need will rarely have attendance problems. When we care for one another, we declare that the church is a family. When we disciple one another for ministry and growth, we are equipping soldiers for the battle. Every leader must face the tension between how much effort to put into caring for people and how much time to spend on developing them. Intentional shepherding occurs when leaders encourage group members to consistently practice both. The Scripture says, "Encourage one another and build each other up" (1 Thess. 5:11).

3. *Build authentic relationships.* Groups often struggle to define their relational purpose. "Do we concentrate on building friendships, or do we focus on accountability?" The answer is, "Yes!" It is both. We all want friends—people to laugh and cry with, people to socialize with, people to simply hang out with. But friendship without accountability produces little spiritual growth. Good friends really care about us, challenge our thinking, and remind us to maintain our commitments. Great examples of this dynamic are found between Jonathan and David (1 Sam. 20) and between Jesus and his disciples (John 15:9–17).

4. *Encourage healthy conflict.* No one enjoys working through conflict. In fact, most of us will do anything to avoid it, hoping the problem will go away. The real question is, "How do we deal with relational problems without destroying the community we are trying to build?" Some people consistently respond with kindness when there is a relational breakdown. They hope that treating the offender nicely—and never pointing out the offense or pattern of sin—will somehow erase the problem. Others prefer head-to-head confrontation, eagerly pointing out someone's error and demanding repentance and contrition. Kindness and confrontation joined together promote reconciliation and create an environment for facing difficult issues with truth and grace (Eph. 4:25–32).

5. *Enjoy serving together.* Humility and spiritual growth are fostered when group members unite to serve others. Groups in which members serve together tend to form stronger bonds of community than those that meet merely for Bible study and prayer. Something amazing happens when group members serve together in loving relationships. Community is developed and the task is accomplished. Task-focused groups will need to emphasize community building, and home groups will need to identify ways to serve those outside the group or outside the church.

6. *Create an inclusive community.* God has called us to love one another (John 13:35) and to reach out to a lost world (Matt. 28:18–20), which requires a group to create intimacy while practicing openness. Remember that there are still many people in your church and outside its walls who need a loving community. If we hoard what we have or fail to love one another as brothers and sisters, we fail to achieve what God has commanded.

When small groups seek to weave all six of these components into the fabric of the community experience, God seems to pour out his love and blessing upon everyone. It's an amazing thing to watch.

Use the table below as a tool to jot down at least one idea or strategy for making progress in each area *as a group*. Your group might not focus on all six of these development themes right now. Give it a try and see what you can brainstorm.

Two key factors that affect growth: group stages and group communication

Using the process, structure, and strategy just listed will help you build a spiritual greenhouse in which group members grow into disciples of Christ. But there are two additional factors that cannot be ignored as you build the greenhouse.

Groups are like families. They move through a variety of growth stages and rely on clear, consistent communication to function well over the long

STRATEGY FOR GROUP GROWTH	
Purpose to Achieve	**Strategy for Group Growth**
Spiritual transformation	
Intentional development	
Authentic relationships	
Healthy conflict	
Serving together	
Inclusive community	

haul. Understanding these stages and group communication patterns will make you aware of the shifting dynamics of group life.

Group stages

Groups, like all living organisms, move through stages of development. The table on pages 100–101 will help you prepare for each stage. Often leaders take the blame for changes in group dynamics that are, in reality, simply the result of a shift to a new stage of the group's life cycle. Use this table to take a snapshot of your group and to plan a strategy for moving productively through each stage.

As you and the group move through these stages, feel free to talk about what is happening, what folks are feeling, and what changes can be made, and agree to work together.

Forming Stage. New groups gather, begin to connect, and people get to know one another. Generally, this is a positive "honeymoon stage" for a group.

Norming Stage. Groups discuss ground rules (covenant), set expectations, define mission or goals, and "do group" together.

Storming Stage. (Crucial stage for the group. Some group experts refer to this period as "transition," and often a group arrives at this place more than once over its life cycle.) The honeymoon is over. People begin to express differences of opinion, wonder about other members, might have some minor conflict or dissatisfaction, long to go deeper, or need to name reality about their feelings. Here a group decides to (1) be a real community, enter the chaos, own the process, accept one another's flaws and quirks, love one another, and get to work, or (2) stay stuck or withdraw to pseudo-community, pretending all is well, never really sharing deeply, and just going through the routines of group life but never really growing beyond basic head knowledge.

Performing Stage. The group rolls up its sleeves and gets to work. Some group experts refer to this as the "work" or "action" phase of a group. People are on mission and engaging relationally, speaking the truth in love, working out differences and disagreements, growing in love for God and others, and making progress in line with the vision and values they created earlier.

Reproduction Stage. Some groups develop an apprentice or two, add people, and eventually spin off another group. They may simply bring in new potential leaders, train them, and send them out to start new groups.

HELPING GROUP MEMBERS PROCESS GROWING PAINS

Stage	Core Stages				Other Stages	
	Forming	Norming	Storming	Performing	Launching	Termination
Number of Meetings per Stage	4–6	6–10	4–8	12–24	4–8	2–6
Members' Questions	Who is in the group? Do I like my group?	Do I fit here? How is our group doing?	Are we really open with each other? Will this group accomplish its mission?	How will we do this? What can we accomplish together? Will we take the risk?	Will we survive? How will we change?	Did we grow? What did we learn? Will I join another group?
Members' Feelings	Excited Expectant Awkward	Comfortable Relaxed Open	Tense Anxious Impatient Doubtful	Eager Open Vulnerable Supportive	Grieved Enthusiastic Mournful Expectant Afraid	Respectful Reflective Thankful Sad
Members' Role	Gather information about others	Give information Accept others	Provide feedback Express frustration	Express feelings Use my gifts Take ownership Accept challenges	Express concerns Accept reality Discuss changes Give blessing	Show love Express thanks Affirm relationships
Leader's Response	Caring Clear Accepting	Affirm Give feedback Exude warmth Model Christlikeness	Confront Encourage Challenge	Challenge Affirm Guide Release	Listen actively Acknowledge feelings Affirm members	Review Reflect Respond
Leader's Role	Communicate vision Promote sharing Define goals	Generate trust Discuss values Facilitate relationships Create covenant	Provide self-disclosure Reexamine covenant Be flexible	Provide service opportunities Clarify goals Begin seeking second apprentice Celebrate results	Cast vision Pray for launch Create subgroups Communicate with apprentice	Celebrate Give gifts Celebrate communion Bring closure

Stage	Core Stages				Other Stages	
	Forming	**Norming**	**Storming**	**Performing**	**Launching**	**Termination**
Content of Communication	Events Topics Facts	Topics People Group God's nature	Personal thoughts Feelings Values God's plan	Group relationships Tasks God's work	People Leadership Vision God's desires	Relationships People God's blessings
Style of Communication	Responsive General Brief	Descriptive Social Explanatory	Assertive Argumentative Directive One-way	Speculative Cooperative Interactive Two-way Confrontive	Interactive Confrontive Expressive	Reflective Understanding Affirming

Termination Stage. Either by design or by simple recognition of reality, almost all groups will come to an end. Processing an ending is very important. Do not neglect this. Celebrate the good things, the growth, the stories, and the joy. Grieve any losses or disappointments. Agree to learn from this experience, even if the group was hard or not great or just did not work out for people. It's okay. Try again to launch another group, or encourage people to try another kind of group. Don't just stop meeting. Have a final meeting so there is closure. You are going to see most of these people again, maybe every week at church, and you want to end well, without hurt feelings or unresolved issues.

REFLECTION

Stages

If you are currently leading or starting a group, what stage is the group in at this time?

continued on next page

What indicators lead you to believe that this is the stage of development?

How are you preparing for the next stage? What needs to happen before you transition into the next stage of development?

Group communication

Communication is essential to developing healthy relationships, healthy families, and healthy churches. Communication is also essential in small groups. Without proper communication with God and with others, your group will become stagnant and superficial. The following four channels of communication (adapted from Ralph Neighbour, *Where Do We Go from Here?*) characterize the levels of interaction in a small group.

1. *God to group.* People want to hear from God. They seek his will and desire to hear his voice. Take time in your group to be silent and to read the Scriptures. Listen as the Holy Spirit works through the Word of God to convict you and challenge you. Listen for the still, small voice of the Lord as he communicates his purpose for your group or for a particular meeting, through the Spirit, through others, and through his Word.

2. *Group to God.* We not only hear from God; we respond to him. A response can take the form of a prayer, an expression of praise, a reading of Scripture back to God, a song, or a quiet devotion that communicates feelings to God.

3. *Group member to group member.* Vulnerable, authentic, truthful communication among group members will enable your group to become a powerful vehicle for life change. Groups grow when members express feelings, words of encouragement, or hurts to one another. Jesus said, "You will know the truth, and the truth will set you free" (John 8:32). Groups characterized by truth telling are groups that experience freedom in Christ. Groups avoid becoming superficial and pretentious when members speak loving, caring truths to one another.

4. *Group to world.* It is our responsibility as believers to take the message of Christianity to a lost and dying world. As groups, we proclaim the truth as we have opportunity to speak with people who might not yet be connected to God. We proclaim the truth both verbally and through our deeds. Reflect on how your group will take action to deliver the message of Christianity to your community and to the world.

ADDITIONAL RESOURCES

Henry Cloud and John Townsend, *Making Small Groups Work* (Zondervan, 2003). Great for creating ground rules and for understanding group process and the role of the leader in guiding groups to become safe and authentic.

Todd Hunter and Eugene Peterson, *Christianity beyond Belief* (InterVarsity, 2010). Hunter provides a very engaging look into the life of discipleship and asks the question, What if you were going to live tomorrow?

Neil McBride, *How to Lead Small Groups* (NavPress, 1990). Chapters 3, 4, and 5 are helpful for leaders seeking to better understand how groups form and grow through various stages of development.

Jenn Miller and Tara Peppers, *Finding the Flow* (InterVarsity, 2008). Focuses on being guided by the Holy Spirit as you lead a group; provides spiritual and relational exercises a group can do together.

Bill Search, *Simple Small Groups* (Baker, 2008). Helps group leaders focus on the core of what small groups are all about, avoiding the many distractions that take leaders off course and make group life more complex and cluttered than God intended.

Chapter 5

LEADING LIFE-CHANGING MEETINGS

Small group meetings can be exciting or frustrating—often at the same time! The possibilities are endless when you consider all the personalities and dynamics represented in a group. Whether you experience chaos or community may depend on any number of factors. You cannot control everything, but you can do many things to invite the powerful work of the Holy Spirit among your people in a meeting.

In this chapter, we will help you prepare for a meeting and understand the various group dynamics. There are a number of skills you'll need for leading a group effectively. Don't feel overwhelmed. You don't have to master them all right away. We have also included some materials to help you put these leadership skills into practice. Finally, we have some tools you can use to evaluate your group and your leadership, providing you with the feedback you need along the way. Get ready to turn small group meetings into exciting moments in which you witness Christ at work, building his church.

MEETING PREPARATION

Focused hard work on meeting preparation and planning will make your group much more effective and successful. Preparation accomplishes three things:

1. Communicates to members that you have a sense of direction and leadership
2. Gives the group confidence in your overall leadership
3. Allows you to alter the course of a meeting (if necessary), because you can make choices regarding what issues you will cover during the meeting

Setting the Stage for an Effective Meeting

1. Carefully think through the Meeting Planner worksheet (described on page 107).
2. Make sure everyone knows where and when the meeting will take place.
3. If you have a host or hostess, contact him or her about details for the meeting.

A host or hostess should

- create a warm, caring atmosphere;
- make sure the logistics (refreshments, seating, and so on) have been accounted for;
- greet people as they enter the room.

Designing an Effective Meeting

Russ Robinson, my ministry partner and friend, has often used four key questions or themes to organize the content of a meeting. This serves as a guide for the entire meeting and especially for how you use the Bible. The "Head, Hands, Heart, and Homework" approach will help you shape the discussion and action components of a meeting. Here are the four questions.

Head. What do I want group members to know or understand?
Heart. What do I hope group members will feel or experience?
Hands. What are we going to do together with what we know?
Homework. What is the assignment for activity or relationships between meetings?

DESIRED OUTCOME	
Head *What do I want group members to know or understand?* The list of spiritual gifts in Romans 12, 1 Corinthians 12, Ephesians 4	**Heart** *What do I hope group members will feel or experience?* Prized by God and each other for their uniqueness
Hands *What are we going to do together with what we know?* The gifts assessment in the Network handbook	**Homework** *What is the assignment for activity or relationships between meetings??* How they expect to begin using their gifts

Meeting Planner and Meeting Preparation Checklist

Now that you have thought through "Head, Heart, Hands, and Homework," create a plan for the meeting. On the following pages, you will find two tools that will help you structure your next meeting: the Meeting Planner and the Meeting Preparation Checklist.

The Meeting Planner

The Meeting Planner (p. 108) guides you as you think through the overall purpose of your group. This planner is a tool to help frame your meeting. Notice that in the Sample Meeting Planner (p. 109), there's a five-minute gap after 7:25. This little extra space allows you to shift focus, grab a piece of cake, update latecomers, and move into another space (from the kitchen, for example, into the living room). There is a twenty- to twenty-five-minute time built into the end of the meeting schedule, for personal visiting with individual members, side conversations, and having that "meeting after the meeting" that often happens.

This is a framework for planning, not a rigid guideline. What if Kevin arrives and, although it's his birthday this week, he tells us he has been having real problems with an employee and today he had to fire the man? The employee has two kids and a sick wife, and Kevin feels awful. Or what if the Bible discussion goes deeper than expected, and some members open their hearts to God's work?

The Holy Spirit is the official leader of the group. The curriculum, experiences, activities, agenda, and our leadership—especially our leadership—are tools in his hands. By having a framework or agenda, we know what to say yes to and what to say no to, what can be dropped or added, what can wait until next meeting and what is urgent for today, and what can be handled offline, between meetings.

The Meeting Preparation Checklist

The Meeting Preparation Checklist is a brief checklist to prompt your thinking and help you remember details. The checklist uses the acronym PLAN, which stands for:

- Purpose of the meeting
- Logistics to be managed
- Activities and work to be done
- Needs of members and others

Once you have used the Meeting Preparation Checklist a few times, you will be able to plan a meeting as you think through PLAN in your head.

MEETING PLANNER

Date_____	Details	Who's Responsible	Time	Comments or Issues
Purpose				
Logistics				
Activities				
Needs				

SAMPLE MEETING PLANNER

Date _Jan. 11_	Details	Who's Responsible	Time	Comments or Issues
Purpose (Head, Heart, Hands, Homework)	To help members understand spiritual gifts and why they are needed.	Kim and I will discuss this on the phone.		Encourage people to take assessment and GIFTS class; pray each day for Spirit to empower us; know gifts of others.
Logistics	Meet at Kim's; cake for Kevin's birthday	Cake: Mike and Sandy Kim: email reminder		Ask everyone to write a note for Kevin.
Activities	1. Birthday & notes 2. Life story — Mike 3. Bible — 1 Cor. 12 4. Prayer — gifts/needs 5. End then move to personal time/ updates ** Discuss new curriculum	1. Kim to lead 2. Mike 3. Me and Kim 4. Kim to lead 5. Me and Kim ** Me: curriculum	7–7:15 7:15–25 7:30–8 8–8:20 8:20–45 8:45–9:00	1. Everyone will read their note. 3. Determine who handles what questions. 4. Focus is on gifts, then shift to personal needs and community. 5. Check in with members. ** Hand out copies of new study guide to prep for next week.
Needs	The Harrises still looking for work.	Group prayer		Update this based on prayer time and personal connections at end of meeting.

The checklist is fairly self-explanatory. If you have questions on how to use it or how it applies to your particular kind of group or ministry, consult your coach or ministry leaders.

CHOOSING THE RIGHT CURRICULUM

Choosing a curriculum can be an overwhelming task, considering the number of options now found in bookstores and online. The Choosing a Curriculum Flowchart on page 114 was designed to help you sift through the myriad of materials to find something your group needs.

A Few Tips about Curriculum

1. *Curriculum is a tool.* Curriculum can never lead the group. Don't forfeit opportunities for extended prayer or service, or cut short a necessary community-building activity, because "we have to get through the curriculum." Jesus did not say, "Go therefore into all the world and complete the curriculum!" Your goal is ultimately to make disciples—Christ followers—who are obedient to Jesus, yielded to the Spirit, and loving toward others.

2. *Curriculum is not intended as a substitute for the Bible.* Curriculum and study guides should be used to enhance the group's purpose and move people toward biblical truth.

3. *Don't feel obligated to finish all the questions.* Competent leaders know what questions to use and how many of them to use. If a curriculum has too many questions, choose a few good ones (five to seven questions at most). Many times, two to three good questions followed by the right kind of group process are more than enough. Better to have a great discussion while grappling with a few good questions than to answer all the questions at a superficial level. The goal is to engage people with the truth of God's Word as it relates to their own heart and growth.

4. *Make sure the curriculum is group friendly.* Many small group studies are designed for understanding the Bible, not building relationships or generating a deep sense of community and caring. Look closely at not only the questions but also the process. Does the curriculum allow for lots of interaction? Does it ask personal disclosure questions that challenge people to open up and share their lives? Or is it filled with content-based "what" questions, often ignoring personal "why" questions?

Meeting Preparation Checklist (PLAN)

P — Purpose

What will the meeting accomplish?

- ☐ Write out "Head, Heart, Hands, Homework" objectives.
- ☐ Write out the meeting agenda on meeting planner.
- ☐ _____
- ☐ _____

L — Logistics

Are the details for the meeting prepared?

- ☐ Seating, lighting, temperature
- ☐ Distractions eliminated (phones, noise, people)
- ☐ Refreshments
- ☐ Music during arrival
- ☐ Childcare arrangements
- ☐ Location of future meeting(s) set
- ☐ _____
- ☐ _____

A — Activities

What is the agenda and work to be done?

- ☐ Discussion starter, social mixer
- ☐ Group prayer and worship
- ☐ Social time or structured exercise/project (materials needed)
- ☐ Bible discussion time
- ☐ Announcements to be made
- ☐ _____
- ☐ _____

N — Needs

What are our concerns for members or others?

- ☐ Unresolved relational problems
- ☐ Financial needs
- ☐ Tough decisions to make
- ☐ Health concerns
- ☐ Family issues
- ☐ _____
- ☐ _____

5. *Look for engaging application questions.* An application section that simply asks, "How would this apply to your life?" is weak. If the writer says something like, "It's clear from this passage that we need to share our faith with others. And it is clear that we all know how and that it would please God. But let's talk about why it is so hard for you and me to start spiritual conversations with seekers. Are there fears or other barriers you face in communicating the gospel? How does it feel when you picture yourself talking to an unsaved person about Christ?" these questions will probe people's motives, thoughts, feelings, and needs. Only then can we truly encourage and pray for one another.

Key Questions When Choosing a Curriculum

What is our purpose?

The curriculum should support the purpose of the group. This purpose may change as the group moves through seasons of growth, maturity, and experience. If a group starts as a grief support group for those who have lost loved ones, the curriculum should reflect that purpose. As people move through the stages of grief, a leader may see that the group members need to understand more about God. As a result, a curriculum on the attributes of God may be appropriate.

Where is the group spiritually?

It is wise to take the spiritual pulse of your group to determine the level of curriculum appropriate for it. If the group is dominated by people investigating the claims of Christ, make sure the questions are appropriate for them. Listen without making rash judgments, don't appear to have all the answers, and deal with the issues facing them as explorers of the faith. Allow them to process information, ask hard questions, and raise objections. Use a Bible version that is easy for them to read and use. *The Journey* from Zondervan, designed with questions and insights for spiritual seekers, is a great Bible for this kind of group.

New and growing believers can handle more difficult Bible discussions and are more willing to tolerate religious jargon. Even so, try to avoid using a lot of religious terminology. While believers who have been around the church longer may feel comfortable with terms like *redemption* or *justification*, avoid using them too much with newer Christ followers unless you expect to spend the time to adequately explain what those terms mean.

What are our key needs?

This question relates to the purpose question but allows a group to address real needs and still accompish the purpose of the group. For example, couples in a group may desire growth in their marriage relationships. Their group may actually be a serving group designed to help meet needs at a local homeless shelter. As couples, they could meet for thirty minutes prior to serving together for a brief study and discussion about marital issues.

What is our current focus?

Sometimes we choose a curriculum based on needs but fail to consider the long-range vision for the group. Your group may be completing a study on Christianity in the workplace. Now some in your group want to study the book of Galatians. Why? How does this fit with the overall group direction for the coming year? Are there elements in Galatians that would be appropriate to focus on, or would it be better to study this book when it makes more sense in the life cycle of the group?

Try to provide a flow unless the situation dictates an abrupt change in focus. For example again, let's suppose your group is completing a personal growth curriculum. Now it might be appropriate to identify one of the areas covered in that book and do an extended series or study on it. A section on finances, for instance, could be expanded to deal with using finances in a compassionate way to help the poor. This would be a great step toward casting a vision for serving others and would not appear to be an abrupt curriculum change.

What are our limitations?

Don't waste your time looking at curriculum designed for a two-hour study when your group has only forty minutes to meet each week. Make sure you have considered the time, location (are you in a distracting environment?), and size of your group (four people can deal with more questions than nine can, assuming you want to allow everyone to participate).

What is the best curriculum?

The curriculum is your servant, not your master. Use it to help people grow. Regularly evaluate and adjust your expectations. Set it aside if it gets in the way. Focus on integrating biblical truths with life development, and you won't be disappointed. Regardless of your approach—Scripture study, topical, or sermon questions—you won't go wrong if you apply truth to life.

Choosing a Curriculum Flowchart

What Is Our Purpose?
- Bible knowledge
- Spiritual disciplines
- Strong relationships
- Caregiving
- Processing life's issues

Where Is the Group Spiritually?
- Seekers
- New believers
- Maturing believers
- Mixed

What Are Our Key Needs?
- Discipleship
- Encouragement
- Obedience
- Marriage enrichment
- Knowledge

What Is Our Current Focus?
- Service
- Gender issues
- Workplace
- Marriage
- Understanding Scripture
- Relationship building

What Are Our Limitations?
- Time
- Location
- Size of group
- Duration of group

What Is the Best Curriculum?
- Scripture passage
- Topic centered/Issue centered
- Book of the Bible
- Church-provided study
- Book with study guide
- Curriculum series
- Sermon-based study

GROUP DYNAMICS

When conducting a meeting, it's important to always be aware of the dynamics of a group. This requires paying attention to the kinds of roles people play in groups, their individual learning styles and personalities, and their spiritual gifts. The interaction of these factors makes each group unique.

Group Roles

Often members take on certain roles (sometimes consciously and sometimes without really knowing they are doing it). People will take on different roles at different stages of your group. Below are some supportive and destructive group roles you might want to be aware of.

Supportive roles

1. *Information seeker.* Asks other members to tell more of their story.
2. *Opinion seeker.* Takes an active interest in what others in the group think.
3. *Initiator.* Offers new ideas, new ways of doing things. Often sets the pace in a discussion.
4. *Elaborator.* Wants more than just the facts in a story. Adds color to the discussion.
5. *Tension reliever.* Often uses gentle humor to relieve tense situations. Uses identification to keep the tense person from feeling alone: "I understand. I feel that way many times myself."
6. *Reviewer.* Tends to provide summary statements and clarity statements.
7. *Consensus seeker.* Looks to see what the group is thinking and whether there is agreement on issues or decisions.
8. *Encourager.* Finds ways to build up others in the group.
9. *Standard bearer.* Holds forth the values of the group and defends them.

Destructive roles

1. *Aggressor.* Insults and criticizes others. May show strong jealousy.
2. *Rabbit chaser.* Consistently focuses on stories or issues irrelevant to the topic at hand but very exciting to him or her.
3. *Recognition seeker.* Tends to focus primarily on his or her own achievements or successes.
4. *Dominator.* Monopolizes group interaction. Tries to control discussions.
5. *Special-interest advocate.* Tends to focus on personal pet peeve regardless of the topic or direction of discussion.
6. *Negativist.* Might be a perfectionist who is never satisfied with anything. Quick to point out the downside of any issue or topic.
7. *Quibbler.* Focuses on details. Often loses the forest for the sake of the trees.
8. *Practical joker.* Rather than using humor positively, tends to distract people with jokes and comments. This is often a defense mechanism and is used whenever a discussion gets too personal.

Your job as a leader is not to peg each person in order to figure out what his or her role is. Roles may change from time to time. You simply need to be aware that these kinds of roles exist in a group. Listen with a sensitive spirit and heart to each person. Ask probing questions that help get behind each role. If you have problems working with a particular type of person in your group, consult your coach or ministry leaders for ways to solve the problem and deal with the relationship.

Learning Styles

Educators and trainers of adults often refer to certain learning styles. There are three major types of learning styles utilized by members of your group. An effective leader should use a variety of presentation and discussion techniques in order to communicate effectively to each learner.

Visual learners

These people respond well to charts, diagrams, and other visual stimuli. They tend to like handouts and enjoy parables and stories. They are visual thinkers—that is, they respond well to word pictures and to vivid, descriptive stories that allow them to picture what is happening.

Tips for the leader: Use handouts, newspaper articles, storyboards, paper and crayons, and objects to keep the attention of your visual learners.

Auditory learners

Auditory learners enjoy learning by hearing. They would rather engage in a discussion on an issue than read a book about it. Some of them may be avid readers, but in general they would rather listen to a story than read one.

Tips for the leader: Use subgroups to allow all members to participate in discussions. Allow group members to respond verbally to questions and decisions. Use background music during prayer times or at the beginning of the meeting.

Kinesthetic learners

These folks like to touch and feel things. They like to participate in the action. They learn by doing. While a visual learner might be motivated to help the poor by seeing a picture of a poor person in an issue of a news magazine, the kinesthetic learner would be motivated by a field trip to the inner city.

Tips for the leader: Utilize objects and experiences for your group. Plan outings and events that allow members to experience truth in action. Allow kinesthetic learners to learn by trial and error, rather than simply telling them the answers.

In order to understand how each member of your group learns and how his or her style interacts with those of others in the group, encourage each member to take the Small Group Insights assessment and then discuss it as a group. You can find it at *www.SmallGroupInsights.com*. Use the code DRBILL when you sign up for the assessment, to receive a special rate.

Personalities: God Made Us All Different!

The purpose of this book is not to help you identify each person's personality in some technical sense. Rather, please understand that people in your group are wired differently. Again, do not spend a lot of time trying to peg each person in your group to a particular personality type. Simply be aware of the tendencies of each personality that might be in your group.

Below is a series of questions you might ask as you think of each group member.

1. Do they tend to be more introverted or extroverted? Does extensive interaction with people tend to energize them (extroverted) or drain them (introverted)?

2. Do they experience life with their senses or more intuitively? Do they make insightful judgments about the way life is and how it functions, or do they tend to seek experiences in which they can taste, touch, see, smell, and hear what is happening around them?

3. Do they initially process information and decisions with their head or with their heart? Some people are more logical and cognitive (head), while others are feelers who tend to respond more emotionally (heart).

4. Do they approach life in a structured or unstructured fashion? That is, are they more likely to plan out each day of a family vacation before they leave the house, or are they more likely to rent a car and decide along the way?

Helping Members Use Their Spiritual Gifts in Your Group

Here is a process for helping people deploy their spiritual gifts in your small group. It will help the group function more effectively and allow each member to grow and mature in his or her area of giftedness.

1. *Cast a vision for mutual ministry.* Together you should read and study Ephesians 4:11 – 13 and 1 Corinthians 14:26. Help your group understand the value of serving others together and serving one another.

2. *Help members identify their gifts.* Encourage people to use spiritual gift assessment tools or classes offered by the church.

3. *Discuss giftedness with each other.* Ask group members to explain their gifts to the group and how they might use them to encourage other members of the group.
4. *Serve in areas of giftedness.* Allow people to serve according to areas of giftedness and passion within your small group.
5. *Consider ministry opportunities.* Discuss ministry opportunities, outside the group, that will utilize people's giftedness.

The Role of the Holy Spirit in Group Dynamics

We have already seen how the Holy Spirit has gifted each member of the group so that the group functions as a body. However, he also works in other ways. He guides people and teaches them from the Word. He can also work through promptings and experiences. As a group leader, be sensitive to the working of the Holy Spirit as he moves among group members. Here are a few suggestions that will help you be open and sensitive to his leading.

1. Pray that the Holy Spirit would do his work of conviction and teaching during your group meeting.
2. Be sensitive to group consensus. If the members sense that there should be a change in direction, this may be the voice of the Spirit. Don't automatically assume that your agenda is the right agenda.
3. If you sense a strong conviction from the Spirit of God to discuss a certain matter or issue, feel free to tell this to the group. Don't force the group to agree with you. Rather, simply explain that you sense that God wants you to share some feelings or issues. Then allow the group and the Word of God to guide you as you move forward.
4. Allow time for the Holy Spirit to work. Sometimes it's best to wait if there is no consensus on an issue. Ask members to pray and to seek the will of God. Allow God's Spirit to work within people over time.

Remember, the Holy Spirit wants to edify and unite a group. This does not mean that all members will agree on all issues. However, it does mean that members of the group should be willing to submit to one another as they seek consensus, understanding that this consensus is likely the result of the Spirit of God working among them to develop community and mutuality. In all cases, verify promptings of the Spirit through the teaching of the Bible. Where the Word of God is clear, obey. Where the Scriptures are silent, seek the will of God and the group consensus as each person submits his or her agenda to Christ and is willing to compromise for the sake of the group.

SKILLS

Icebreakers and Group Openers

Using group openers is a basic yet essential small group skill. Icebreaker ideas and share questions are designed to facilitate discussion about members' personal lives and to help members open up more freely. They are not designed for simple yes or no answers.

Use discretion with these questions and statements. Some will evoke deep and serious responses. Others are light and funny. If your group is new, you should probably use questions and icebreakers that focus on information about people's lives (where they grew up, where they went to school, how they came to your church, where they work, what they think about certain events in our culture, and so on). As intimacy develops in a group, begin to challenge people with more in-depth questions that evoke feelings, thoughts, and insights.

"What is your favorite movie and why?"

"If money were no problem, and you could choose one place in the world to travel to for a week, what would that place be and why?"

"Write down your two most favorite summer activities. Pair off and share those activities with one another, explaining why they are your favorites."

"Who is your number one advisor in life and why?"

"One of my biggest pet peeves is _____."

"People might be surprised to find out that I _____."

"You have three wishes. What would you wish for?"

"If you suddenly lost your eyesight, what one thing would you miss seeing the most?"

"What is the most daring thing you have ever done? What made it so daring?"

"My favorite way to waste time is _____."

"You have one minute to speak to the entire nation on national television. What one or two key things would you like to tell the people of this country?"

"What's the story behind the longest time you've gone without sleep?"

"What were the circumstances that surrounded your first kiss?"

"Who is the most famous person you've known or met? How did it happen?"

"When I dated, I was considered _____ because _____."

"If you could do one miracle (other than make the whole world Christian), what would you do? Why?"

"What do you miss most about childhood?"

"What's the biggest lie you ever told?"

"If given a choice, how would you choose to die? How do you *not* want to die?"

"What is your biggest fear about death?"

"If you could go to college (or go to college again), what would you study?"

"What's the worst storm or disaster you've been in? What was it like?"

"Decribe the most boring day or event or period of time you can remember."

"What day of your life would you most like to relive? Why?"

"What's the smallest space you've lived in? What was it like?"

"In high school, I was (or would have been) voted 'most likely to _____.'"

"Just for the fun or thrill of it, before I die I'd like to _____."

"My number two career choice would be _____."

"As a time traveler, I would most like to visit _____ because _____."

"What was one of the greatest adventures you have ever been on?"

"If I could invent a gadget to make my life easier, I'd invent something that would _____ because _____."

"Next year looks better to me because _____."

"Next year may be a problem because _____."

"I am most like my mom in that I _____."

"I am most like my dad in that I _____."

"I wish that before I got married, someone had told me _____."

"I have never quite gotten the hang of _____."

"I'm a bundle of nerves or all thumbs when it comes to _____."

"I will probably never _____, but it would still be fun if I could."

"What are a couple of things you remember about your grandparents?"

"What does your name mean? Why were you named that?"

"What is one of the most memorable dreams you have ever had?"

"If you were going to leave the world one piece of advice before you died, what would you say?"

"If you were to describe yourself as a flavor, what flavor would you be?"

"What was the best gift you ever received as a child?"

"If you could raise one person from the dead, who would you raise and why?"

"Who was one of the most interesting persons you or your family ever entertained?"

"What is the nicest thing anybody ever said about you?"

"What one thing would you like your obituary to say about you? Why?"

"What is your favorite city? Why?"

"Where do you go or what do you do when life gets too heavy for you? Why?"

"Which do you value most—sight or speech? Why?"

"When you were growing up, who was the neighborhood bully? What made that person so frightening?"

"What is your fondest memory of a picnic? Why was it so special?"

"What is the best news you have heard this week? The worst news?"

"What was one of the worst things your brother or sister did to you as a child?"

"If your house were on fire, what three items (not people) would you try to save?"

"What was your first job? What do you remember most about it?"

"Who was the best boss you ever had? What made him or her so good?"

"When you were a child, what did you want to be when you grew up? What did your parents want you to be?"

"If you could choose one way to do your wedding differently (parachuting while reciting your wedding vows, holding the ceremony underwater, and so on), what would you choose?"

"Who was your hero when you were growing up? How did you try to imitate him or her?"

"If you could go on national television and warn your countrymen to avoid three things, what would you say?"

"What was your worst boss like?"

"I suspect that behind my back, people say I'm _____ because _____."

"Tell the group briefly the story of your wedding day." (If you give them advance notice, each couple can bring their pictures to share with the group.)

"Tell the group what's been happening in your life lately, using the following categories: something old, something new, something happy, something blue."

"Why do you sin?" (No simplistic answers allowed!)

"In what area of your life would you like to have greater peace? Why?"

"If you could someday have a worldwide reputation for something, in what area would you like that to be? Why?"

"What is one of your biggest fears about the future?"

"Using a fruit or vegetable as a metaphor, how would you describe your life this week (dried fig, ripe cantaloupe, smashed banana, and so on)?"

"What do you like best about children? Why?"

"Of the things money can buy, what do you long for the most?"

"If you had to go to prison for a year, what do you imagine would be the hardest part of that experience? Why that?"

"Describe a grade school teacher who made a big impression on you (for good or ill)."

"You have been granted one hour with the president of the United States. What would you ask? What would you like to say?"

"You have been given a one-year sabbatical from work. You can't go more than 150 miles for any leg of the journey. What would you do along the way at each place you stop?"

"Break your life into three equal segments. What was the most significant event from each of these periods of time?"

Have each person in the group answer for every other member of the group: "I am so glad God made you _____ because that aspect of who you are is _____."

"Something I have from my childhood I'll probably never give up is _____ because _____."

"The most useless thing in my (our) house is _____, but it's still there because _____."

"The thing in my wallet (or purse) that tells the most about who I think I really am is _____ because _____."

"When you were a child, what was your favorite time of day? Day of the week? Time of the year? Why were these favorites?"

"In general, people worry too much about _____."

"I want to be taken more seriously in the following area: _____."

"An emotion I often feel but don't usually express is _____."

Facilitating Dynamic Discussion

Four facilitator actions

A leader ACTS to facilitate discussions by:

- *Acknowledging everyone who speaks during a discussion.* Even if several people speak at once, make sure to recognize each one. Also, respond to laughter or a groan or a deep sigh—remember, 90 percent of communication is nonverbal.

- *Clarifying what is being said and felt.* Say, "Let me see if I understand what you are saying."
- *Turning it back to the group as a means of generating discussion.* Don't be the answer person. Ask, "What do others of you think about what was just said?"
- *Summarizing what has been said.* Offer statements like, "So far, it seems like we have been saying ..." or "Nancy, could you try to summarize the key components of the discussion so far?"

Questions

Another key to facilitating dynamic discussions is generating the right kinds of questions and offering appropriate responses. Here are some guidelines for the kinds of questions and responses that will help your group engage in meaningful, challenging discussions.

Opening questions

Use an opening question to help the group members warm up to each other, to allow them to get to know one another better, and to let them hear their own voices. Opening questions are speculative and engaging, preparing members' minds and hearts for the topic to be discussed.

You may want to broach the topic of discussion with a short, creative illustration or story that will answer the question, Why do I want to discuss this topic tonight? Examples of opening questions:

"What do you look forward to as you grow older?"
"What often drives us to fear intimacy with one another? What can we do as a group to diminish this anxiety?"

Launching questions

Knowing the goal of the discussion, the group leader prepares launching questions designed to generate group interaction and feedback. These questions are typically designed to answer the questions, "What do I know?" "What do I feel?" "What should I do?" Examples:

"What do we learn from seeing the obstacles Joseph faced and how he overcome them?"
"After hearing tonight's discussion, we all agree that we are somewhat stuck. What steps can we take to develop greater levels of trust with each other?"
"What do you think was going through Peter's mind at this time?"

Some questions do not necessarily launch a discussion, but they do solicit responses and feedback. There are two kinds of launching questions: those that are leading and those that are limiting.

Leading questions usually produce a short answer:

"Would you be tempted in this situation?"
"Do you agree or disagree with this statement?"

Limiting questions indicate that you have a specific answer in mind. They do not promote much discovery. However, they can help clarify facts.

"What three commands do we find in this passage?"
"What two things does Paul say we must do?"

Guiding questions

Even the most well-prepared leader will need to spontaneously guide discussion at times.

Rephrase the question: "You seem to be asking, 'How can we develop trust as a group?'"
Personalize the question: "How would you respond to Jesus if he asked you that question?"
Test for consensus or decision: "Are we saying that everyone must obey this command?"

Summarizing questions

Summarizing after a series of questions allows the leader to acknowledge group members' contributions while maintaining biblical integrity and direction.

An affirming comment can be made with good eye contact and a smile by saying, "Thanks for sharing that" or "That's a good point" or "Okay, that is a response worth considering. Are there other thoughts as well?"
A summarizing response might be, "So what we see in this passage is ..."

Application questions

The goal of the small group study is not just information but also transformation. The leader can help members apply what they have learned, by asking application questions.

"What changes will you make this week as a result of our discussion tonight?"
"What difference does this make to you and me?"

Responses

How you and other members of the group respond to questions or statements will either foster or fizzle discussion. Here are some tips on how to respond appropriately to members' questions or comments.

Affirming responses

These responses acknowledge each person's value. They promote intimacy and openness. Such responses send a strong signal to group members, telling them they have been heard, understood, and respected.

"I understand this sharing is painful for you. I'm feeling very sad for the way you were treated by your boss this week."

"Bob, I realize you want to talk, but it's important that we listen to what Steven has shared and try to come alongside him during this critical time of decision for him."

Participatory responses

These responses invite others to join in the discussion. They not only affirm a participant's sharing but also invite others to engage in the process. Participatory responses do not isolate group members by shaming, embarrassing, or lecturing them.

"How have others in the group dealt with grief you have experienced?"

"Sam, that was a terrific insight; could you share how you came to that realization?"

"Bob has shared some deep feelings tonight. How might others of you have responded to a similar confrontation at work?"

Paraphrasing or "going deeper" responses

Paraphrasing allows you to repeat the thoughts of others and enables them to share more deeply. It summarizes what has been heard and allows the group to explore personal feelings, thoughts, and actions.

"June, if I heard you correctly, I believe you stated something similar to what Keri shared last week. Do you share the same feelings as Keri on this matter?"

"That was a very painful episode in your childhood, wasn't it, Greg? How did you deal with it? How do you face it today?"

"It is exciting to be part of a victory like you shared, Sharon. How does that impact your relationship with your husband, Scott?"

These kinds of responses—affirming, participatory, and paraphrasing—will enable you to value your members while encouraging them to express feelings, thoughts, and personal concerns.

GROUP PRAYER

What Can I Do to Facilitate Meaningful Prayer in My Group?

Model it

1. Be a person of prayer yourself—pray for your members and for who might fill the open chair, asking God to give you his direction in leading the group.
2. When you pray out loud in the group, keep your prayers honest, authentic, and from your heart.
3. Basic guide for group prayer:

   - Short prayers create safety.
   - Simple prayers are direct and honest.
   - Spirit-led prayers rely on God's power.
   - Silent prayers are okay for anyone, especially newcomers.

Keep it safe

1. Don't call on someone to pray unless you've asked permission beforehand (or you know them well).
2. Don't expect everyone to pray every time.
3. Try to avoid praying in a circle. Allow members to pray one at a time as they feel led.
4. Respect the intimacy level. As the group grows in deepening relationships, a sense of safety will foster a deeper experience in prayer.
5. Be clear on who will close the prayer time.

Guide the prayer

1. Give guidelines, but let the Holy Spirit lead.
2. Avoid lengthy discussions on prayer.
3. Include prayer each time you meet.
4. Use a variety of praying methods.

What Happens When Group Members Commit to Pray for One Another?

- Your relationship with Christ and with each other will deepen. You will experience spiritual growth.

- There is less chance of burnout as you put problems in God's hands and trust members to his care.
- You allow the Holy Spirit to work in your group so your time together is filling and refreshing.
- God will answer your prayers in amazing ways, and your faith will increase.

Creative Ideas for Group Prayer

1. Pray through a psalm out loud together.
2. In a couples' group, have spouses pray for each other.
3. Vary prayer time among the beginning, middle, and closing of the meeting.
4. Pick a portion of Scripture to pray for one another during the week (for example, Col. 1:9 or Eph. 3:14–19).
5. Pray through your church's prayer requests given in the bulletin or program each week.
6. If someone is in crisis, stop right then and pray for him or her.
7. Pray for the church, a country, a family in need, specific seeker-oriented events, or any area for which your group has a passion.
8. Do a study on prayer. Highly recommended: *Praying from God's Heart* by Lee Braise, *Prayer* by Richard Foster, or *Too Busy Not to Pray* by Bill Hybels.
9. Is there someone in your group with the gift of faith or encouragement? Ask that person to be the prayer coordinator, who writes down requests each meeting and keeps track of answers. If a group member has an emergency, he or she can call the prayer coordinator, who will notify all the other members to pray for that person.
10. Praise can be a part of intercession. Is a member in the midst of struggle? Praise God in the struggle (see Psalm 13).
11. Have each member write down requests for the week on a piece of paper, fold the paper, and put it in a hat. Pass the hat, each member agreeing to pray for the person he or she picks and to call to encourage that person during the week.
12. To cut down on the time your group spends talking about prayer requests, give everyone a three-by-five-inch card to write down prayer requests for the week and have them exchange cards with another member of the group.
13. We need to voice our requests from God's perspective and will (John 5:14–15). The next time you are asked to pray for an event, for someone's salvation, or for someone's health, stop and ask your heavenly

Father, "What are your desires, and what can I pray that will cause your desires to take place?"

What to Pray for Others: Colossians 1:9–14

Intercessory prayer can be defined as asking God to act on behalf of someone else. Sometimes we don't know how to pray for our friends and family (or even those who have hurt us), yet we know we should pray for them. In Colossians 1:9–14 Paul gave us a pattern to follow when we pray for others. Read this passage and try using it as a pattern the next time you pray. Watch how God answers.

Pray that

1. they will understand God's will;
2. they gain spiritual wisdom;
3. they live a life pleasing and honoring to God;
4. they do kind things for others;
5. they know God better and better;
6. they are filled with God's strength;
7. they endure in patience;
8. they stay full of Christ's joy;
9. they are always thankful;
10. they recall God's forgiveness of their sins.

Biblical Examples and Styles of Prayer

The Lord's Prayer, which serves as a basic model for us (because it includes several kinds of petitions), and some prayers from Scripture give a wealth of methods, or styles, for moving your group to deeper levels of praying.

Kinds of Prayer

Opening	"Hear our prayer"	Neh. 1:11; Ps. 5:1–3
Adoration	"Hallowed be your name"	Deut. 10:21; 1 Chron. 29:10–13; Ps. 34:8–9
Affirmation	"Your will be done"	Ps. 27:1; Isa. 26:3; Rom. 8:38–39
Group needs	"Give us this day"	Ps. 7:1; Neh. 1:11; Matt. 7:7–8
Confession	"Forgive us our debts as we forgive our debtors"	Ps. 51; Matt. 18:21–22; 1 John 1:9
Renewal (protection)	"Lead us not into temptation"	1 Cor. 10:13

Thanksgiving	"Give thanks to the Lord"	1 Chron. 16:34; Ps. 75:1; Rev. 11:17
Blessing	"The Lord bless you and keep you"	Num. 6:22–27; Ps. 1:1
Commissioning	"Go therefore and make disciples"	Matt. 28:18–20; Acts 1:8
Healing	"The prayer of faith will make well"	James 5:13–16; Ps. 6:2; 41:4
Warfare	"Get behind me, Satan"	Matt. 4:10; 16:23
Closing	"May the grace of the Lord"	2 Cor. 13:14; Eph. 3:20–21

BUILDING RELATIONSHIPS IN THE GROUP

The purpose of relationship-building exercises is to build trust and create friendships in your group by encouraging fun, communication, honesty, transparency, authenticity, and shared experiences. As relationships grow, community will be enhanced.

See appendix 2 for an extensive list of relationship-building exercises. With all of these exercises, please remember:

- Know your goal.
- Think through the group size, and break the group down into subgroups if necessary.
- Make sure you allow enough time for everyone to participate in the exercise.
- The leader must participate like everyone else.
- Let the Spirit move and don't get in the way. Be discerning about when to step in or redirect and when to just be quiet. Face the awkwardness that arises as people express their emotions.

SOCIAL ACTIVITIES

1. Eat meals together.
2. Play sports together.
3. Take a retreat as a group.
4. Go to a park.
5. Go to a concert.
6. Go to a lake for the day.
7. Go someplace special at Christmastime.
8. Go to a pumpkin patch at Thanksgiving.
9. Have a fall harvest party.

10. Watch a video together and critique it.
11. Make popcorn, ice cream, or pizza together.
12. Brainstorm with your group some fun things to do.

CONFLICT MANAGEMENT

As relationships in groups deepen, conflict is inevitable. A group that experiences no conflict is probably either a brand-new group or a group that has not pursued authentic relationships. Let's look at some biblical principles for conflict management and then at some effective conflict management strategies for small group leaders.

Biblical Principles for Conflict Management

The Bible differentiates between quarreling and constructive conflict. Quarreling is negative because it refers to vain arguments or disagreements for the purpose of promoting self-worth or causing division. James 4:1–2 asks us, "What causes fights and quarrels among you? Don't they come from your desires that battle within you? You want something but don't get it. You kill and covet, but you cannot have what you want. You quarrel and fight. You do not have, because you do not ask God" (NIV). This kind of quarreling is not pleasing to God. Paul told Timothy the same thing in 2 Timothy 2:24, which says, "The Lord's servant must not quarrel" (NIV).

However, there is much admonition in Scripture for leaders to use constructive criticism and exhortation in order to bring about spiritual growth. In 2 Timothy 3:16 this is referred to as "rebuking," and in other places as "admonition" or "exhortation."

The Distinction between Quarreling and Constructive Conflict

Quarreling (James 4:2)	Constructive Conflict (Matt. 5:23–26)
seeks win-lose	leads to win-win
tends to divide and to choose sides	seeks to reconcile and to choose steps
exaggerates strife	speaks truth in love
is an end in itself	is a means to an end
tears down	clears path toward something better
usually has a hidden agenda	is only about what is in the open
comes from a person pushing an issue	brought about by necessity in community
is a battle	is work
is usually hard	is usually hard

Strategies for Managing Conflict

There are several approaches to conflict management, each having its own benefits. In small groups, however, the strategies of compromise and collaboration are probably the most effective.

Avoidance

Avoidance is an effective strategy to use with conflict when

- the issue is trivial;
- the situation will take care of itself;
- saving face (yours or someone else's) is important;
- time is limited.

Avoidance is not an effective strategy to use with conflict when

- the problem is important;
- the problem will not resolve itself (and may worsen if neglected);
- credibility will be lost by avoidance;
- there is a larger, underlying issue that is important to address.

Competition

Competition is an effective strategy to use with conflict when

- a competitive interaction will result in a better solution;
- you want one person or position to prevail over another, but you cannot declare your sympathies publicly;
- the issue outweighs the relationship;
- encouraging competition will clarify the issue and expose weak spots.

Competition is not an effective strategy to use with conflict when

- long-term relationships are important;
- conflict is likely to become personal rather than remaining issue oriented;
- it is important to avoid a win-lose situation or public defeat.

Accommodation

Accommodation is an effective strategy to use with conflict when

- the relationship is more important than the task;
- the issue is trivial;
- small concessions will reap further gains (that is, choose your battles).

Accommodation is not an effective strategy to use with conflict when

- your actions could be viewed as condescending;
- its use would set an unwise precedent.

Compromise

Compromise is an effective strategy to use with conflict when

- there is no simple solution;
- both parties have a strong interest in very different facets of the problem;
- there is not enough time for a truly collaborative solution;
- the situation is not critical, and an adequate solution is good enough.

Compromise is not an effective strategy to use with conflict when

- a dangerous precedent will be set by failure to hold one's ground;
- an optimal resolution is possible;
- it is important to avoid concessions of any kind.

Collaboration

Collaboration is an effective strategy to use with conflict when

- the task and the relationship are both very important;
- the time, information, and willingness to collaborate are present;
- the outcome is exceedingly important;
- sufficient trust exists between the parties.

Collaboration is not an effective strategy to use with conflict when

- time, trust, and resources are not available;
- the issue is not worthy of the investment of time, energy, and resources.

Care-Fronting: The Creative Way through Conflict

In his book *Caring Enough to Confront*, David Augsburger describes an approach to conflict management called "care-fronting." The following is a synopsis of that strategy.

Incorrect thinking about caring: Caring *is a good word when confronting is absent.* There is a time for caring, and a person should care when care is called for. But caring dare not be contradicted by any admixture of confrontation. To care genuinely, candor and confrontation must be forgotten, at least for the moment. When someone cares deeply about another person, they cannot confront, because hurting that person is the very last thing they want to do.

Incorrect thinking about confronting: Confronting *is a bad word when compared with caring.* There is a time for confronting, and a person should confront when confrontation is required. But confronting must not be contaminated by any admixture of caring. To confront powerfully, care must be laid aside. When someone is angry, they should confront. To talk of caring at a moment like that would be false.

Correct thinking about caring and confronting: "Care-fronting." Together, the words *care* and *confronting* provide the balance of love and power that lead to effective human relationships. Unfortunately, the more common practice is to keep these distinct and separate.

Care-fronting offers genuine caring that bids another grow. To care is to welcome, invite, and support growth in another. It offers real confrontation that calls out new insight and understanding. To confront effectively is to offer the maximum of useful information with the minimum of threat.

Care-fronting unites love and power and unifies concern for relationship with concern for goals. This way, one can have something to stand for *(goals)* as well as someone to stand with *(relationship)*, without sacrificing one for the other or collapsing one into another. Thus one can love powerfully—and be powerfully loving. These are not contradictory; they are complementary.

Expressing Anger in Groups

There are two ways of expressing anger in groups. "I" messages are clear and confessional. The person using "I" messages owns his or her anger, responsibility, or demands without placing blame. "You" messages are most often attacks, criticisms, labels, devaluation of the other person, or ways of fixing blame.

When angry, try to give clear, simple "I" messages. Following are some examples of "I" and "you" messages.

"I" Messages	"You" Messages
I am angry.	You make me angry.
I feel rejected.	You're judging and rejecting me.
I don't like the wall between us.	You're building a wall between us.
I don't like blaming or being blamed.	You're blaming everything on me.
I want the freedom to say yes or no.	You're trying to run my life.
I want respectful friendship with you again.	You have to respect me, or you're not my friend.

IDEAS FOR WORSHIP

1. Listen to or sing along with a worship tape.
2. Walk through a nearby park or forest preserve and praise God for his creative power.
3. Ask your group to think of the names of God found in Scripture. Ask each member to tell why the name he or she thought of is important, and pause to give God glory for who he is.
4. Ask a few members to select a favorite psalm or Scripture passage that focuses on who God is or who Jesus is. Read each passage aloud and then pause to pray.
5. Have each member write prayers of worship and praise to God. Ask the members to share them with the group. Think of this as writing a letter to God.
6. Go to a worshipful Christian concert or church service together.
7. Have members in your group use their video cameras (if they have one) to record images of things that cause them to think about God or want to worship him. View them together as a group. Pause to reflect upon who God is and what he is doing in your lives.

OUTREACH

1. Pray for someone to fill the open chair.
2. Pray for different parts of the world that need Christ.
3. Pray for a missionary from the church.
4. Plan a trip to the inner city.
5. Gather materials or gifts together to present to an orphanage in America or Mexico.
6. Have a potluck dinner and invite visitors.
7. Have a Superbowl party or Oscar night and invite neighbors.
8. Adopt a child through World Vision and support that child financially.
9. Plan to bring friends to a seeker service.
10. Take the *Becoming a Contagious Christian* training course together.

TROUBLESHOOTING TIPS

Creating safe places where life change can be maximized is not easy. Sometimes it's reassuring to know that all small groups undergo some type of relational difficulty. If group members expect to grow, people will have to be vulnerable. Anyone who has ever led or been a part of a nurturing small group will tell you that where people are emotionally transparent, problems will come to the surface. When they do, it's the leader's job to help steer the group in the right direction.

Two principles guide a leader's attempts at successful troubleshooting. First, any solution must promote the health and wholeness of the individual. Second, any solution must also promote the health and wholeness of the group.

The following troubleshooting tips were garnered in part from discussions with seasoned small group leaders. They should go a long way in helping your group to graciously and insightfully deal with problem situations. Remember, no technique is 100 percent successful in solving the difficulties your group may encounter, but with prayerful attention, sensitivity, and caring interaction using one or more of these tips, your group has a good chance of not only making it through your particular barrier but also realizing true community and maturity on the other side of it.

Issue 1: The Overly Talkative Member

If not moderated properly, what often begins as a trickle of friendly patter can turn into a virtual flood of words. The Talker is rarely shy and usually very uncomfortable with long periods of silence. Typically, what's behind this need to fill in the pauses is the fear of intimacy or personal disclosure. The Talker is quick to move on an item and can easily unsettle a group's pacing if there isn't some type of sensitive intervention. Here are some tools that you may find helpful.

Establish ground rules for your group

- Set the rule that no one can speak a second time unless everyone who wants to talk has had a chance to speak. Often in the case of a Talker who is married, the spouse is silent or appears introverted. Use the situation to your advantage. Each person may speak a second time only after his or her spouse has been given an opportunity. You will be amazed at the positive response from overrun mates.
- Make (or reiterate) the rule that no one can overrun someone else while he or she is speaking (translation: "No interrupting!").
- Go systematically around the group, allowing each person a chance to talk. Remember at the onset to be sensitive with members who are either unaccustomed to speaking in a group setting or feel uncomfortable with it.
- Tell the talkative member privately that you value his or her sharing but wish to hear other people's comments as well. In front of the group, state that you would like to hear more about the person's items of interest after the meeting.

- Agree at the beginning of the meeting to save some issues for the end, after everything else has been discussed (this only works after you have seen the Talker verbally camp on certain subjects repeatedly).
- Here's a creative solution: Throw a football or some other object around the room. Only the person with the object in his or her hand has the right to talk.
- During the discussion, simply interject a question sensitively directed to another person.

Meet individually
- Spend some one-on-one time with the Talker. Try to ascertain the driving issues making it necessary for the person to dominate the meeting.
- Firmly and sensitively confront the person in private. Begin with the positive contributions the person has made in the group and the need for others to be given the opportunity to make a similar impact. Use the confrontation time as an important affirmation moment as well.
- Ask for the Talker's help in drawing others out. Suggest that the person end his or her comments with a question like, "So what do the rest of you think?"

Issue 2: The Answer Person

For too many years within the Christian community, spiritual fruitfulness has been wrongly determined on the basis of how much you know. This measure stands in sharp contrast to the biblical notion that "fruit" for the believer is defined by what you do and who you are. Because of this misinterpretation of Jesus's teaching, knowledge has preceded action on the list of preeminent Christlike virtues. It is not hard to see, then, why many sincere members of a group see nothing wrong with throwing around easy answers, with simply quoting a Bible verse, or with becoming wrapped up in some minute theological trivia having nothing to do with the group discussion. These members are often argumentative and have little tolerance for outside interpretation of feelings or biblical passages. They often will go to great lengths to make sure their opinions are heard and validated.

Answer people all too quickly dismantle safe places. Other members should not have to experience the pain of nonattention, judgment, or an argumentative spirit. Here are some helpful ways to provide what the answer person needs and keep the group process on track.

Take action during the meeting

- Backtrack to the original idea, question, or thought shared.
- Refocus on the passage or material being used, and collect more information from everyone; then summarize.
- Lovingly redirect the discussion to the other group members: "What do the rest of you think of this passage?" or "How do the rest of you feel?"
- Affirm what is right about the "always right" person's answers, but look for other points of view.
- Be a model of true empathy yourself so that the answer person can see a better way to help others.
- Remind the group of the importance of silence.
- Avoid arguing about who is right or wrong.
- Before the meeting, share how pat answers or oversimplified responses make others feel. Ask the group to monitor themselves. Don't feel afraid to call members on this after you have set the ground rules.

Speak to the answer person

- If it's a continuing problem, talk with the person outside the group. Describe to him or her what sharing in this manner does to the group. Tell the truth in love.
- Affirm the person for what he or she knows, but also point out how this knowledge may not be what is needed or appropriate.
- Let the person know that he or she needs to let other people's communication stand on its own, without judgment or immediate correction.
- Ask the insensitive member to share more feelings rather than always sharing thoughts.
- Ask the answer person to help summarize or rephrase points of the discussion.
- Try to find out from the person privately what drives him or her to always appear in the know.

Issue 3: The Member with an Agenda

All of us struggle from time to time with the issue of wanting to maintain inordinate control over aspects of our lives. Groups can become the arena where our sinful power struggles play out. Some individuals will repeatedly try to prove themselves by trying to redirect some facet of group life their way for no apparent reason other than their own preferences.

A person presenting this problem leaves telltale language clues. Look for phrases such as "Yes, but" or "Well, I think." Often this person is critical of the group process, even with items considered tabled by the group. Here are some hints to aid you in dealing with this individual.

Reaffirm group covenants while you're all together
- Reaffirm, recast, reestablish, challenge, redefine—use whatever word you want—but remind everyone of the agreed-upon guidelines for group involvement.
- Discuss these standards with everyone in the group, to affirm the purpose and values of the gathering.

Speak to the person with the agenda
- Confront the person privately and try to discern the underlying problem.
- Suggest that the person work with the other members to find a proactive solution that solves the problem yet doesn't violate the boundary established by the group.

Issue 4: Superficial Discussions

Beginning relationships often have a period in which facts are shared more easily than feelings. Not much is bartered in terms of emotional risk, and therefore not much is gained at this stage. Early on, this surface-level communication is normal and shouldn't be cause for alarm.

Often, though, a group struggles to break through the ice of superficiality and go deeper, even after many meetings. This hesitation can be the result of a leader's direction or can be caused by someone else impeding the bonding process. Whatever is keeping the group in a frozen mode, you can easily prepare yourself to handle this problem.

Surface communication can also be a sign that you are trying to go too deep too fast. Mentally take a step back and ascertain whether this is so. If you sense you have moved too quickly, admit your error and be willing to proceed at a more realistic pace. By humbling yourself in this way, you model vulnerability rather than harming the relational chemistry of the group. Your openness works to center the group's focus and unite the participants for future growth together.

Improve your questions
- By far, the number one way to open up a group is to lead by example. "Speed of the leader, speed of the team" could easily have been first

postulated in a small group. The rule of thumb is to share as deeply and openly as you would like the others to share.

- Have specific applications and questions. Don't be afraid to challenge the group.
- Ask "feeling" questions rather than just "opinion" or "fact" questions.
- Where appropriate, be more directive. Sometimes ask closed-ended questions that will elicit specific answers, rather than open-ended questions.
- Restate and rephrase the question. Often silence means that group members are simply unsure of what was asked of them. (Silence may also indicate that they're thinking, not that they're reluctant.)

Create a safer climate

- During initial minutes of the meeting, remind members of confidentiality guidelines.
- If your group is too large, break into subgroups.
- Contact the group members outside of the meeting to see if anything could have made the questions easier to answer.

ADDITIONAL RESOURCES

Cindy Bunch, *The Small Group Idea Book* (InterVarsity, 2003). A resource filled with great ideas for building community, outreach, creative Bible discussions, projects, and prayer.

Bill Donahue and Russ Robinson, *Walking the Small Group Tightrope* (Zondervan, 2003). Unpacks the six challenges every group leader faces as he or she balances the tension between good ideas and desires in groups. Provides creative strategies for guiding group members through the process of naming group realities and moving forward together to achieve group purposes.

Gordon Fee and Doug Stuart, *How to Read the Bible for All It's Worth* (Zondervan, 2003). An in-depth look at the culture, genre, and literature of the Bible so that readers and Bible students understand the context and culture of the Bible as they read it.

Richard Foster, *Life with God* (Harper, 2010). How to read the Bible for spiritual transformation, not just information.

Steve Gladen, *Small Groups with Purpose* (Baker, 2011). Using the Saddleback experience, Gladen describes how to lead groups that grow people in Christ.

Roberta Hestenes, *Using the Bible in Groups* (Westminster Press, 1983). Creative ways to use the Bible and to study it in a group setting.

Eddie Mosley, *Connecting in Communities* (NavPress, 2011). This resource looks at the overall small group ministry and how to design it so groups function in healthy ways.

Chapter 6

MEASURING GROUP PROGRESS

Every ministry must pause and ask the questions, Are we really effective? Is our ministry making an impact? Are we wisely stewarding the resources God has given us? Are people growing to be more like Christ, acting as he would?

Covering this material now may seem premature, because we have not discussed chapter 7, "Caring for Members," or chapter 8, "Impacting Your World." Should we be assessing progress in those arenas of ministry as well? Of course!

THE VALUE OF FEEDBACK

Providing healthy feedback solves problems and creates closeness and attachment among group members.

Giving feedback means we confront reality—positive and negative. The word *confront* comes from the Latin and means "turn your face toward." Giving feedback is simply turning our faces toward the group and toward one another and asking, "What is working? What is not working? How can we make necessary changes or adjustments and do better?"

Biblical references:

- Psalm 15:2—Speak truth from the heart.
- Proverbs 15:2, 4—Wise people speak with knowledge and bring healing.
- Proverbs 15:23—How good is a timely word.
- Proverbs 16:13—Leaders value people who speak the truth.
- Proverbs 27:6—Wounds (hard words) from a friend can be trusted.
- Ephesians 4:25–29—Put off falsehood (pretense) and speak truth.

Here are some benefits of feedback.

- Promotes change in behavior
- Brings healing to relationships that might be strained
- Solves problems caused by inappropriate behavior, such as straying from the group's vision
- Promotes spiritual, relational, and emotional growth
- Acts as a mirror for the truth about the group and about members
- Promotes wholeness in the group
- Has a containing function—allows you to name and address issues before they become larger problems or frustrations
- Allows you to celebrate what is working and create strategies for doing more of these good things

QUALITATIVE AND QUANTITATIVE MEASUREMENT

What do we measure? Items to evaluate and discuss tend to fall into two large categories—quantitative and qualitative. Quantitative measures include the following examples.

Number of group members
Meeting times and location
Use of materials or study guides
Accomplishing the mission
How often we served outside the group

Qualitative measures deal with the feel and character of the group, whether the process is working, and how relationships are progressing. These tend to be more intangible, subjective, and open to a range of people's opinions. These might include:

Relationships
Processing disagreements or conflicts
Prayer life of the group
Personal growth issues
Overall group satisfaction

Many of you are familiar with the qualitative and quantitative measures from the fields of business or education. Let's take it a step further for your group. Look at these measures *in the context of where they take place—inside the circle or outside the circle*. In this way, you can get a better handle on what needs to change within the group and what needs to change as your group seeks to have impact outside the group (the focus of chapter 8).

So there are external and internal factors that can be observed to measure performance or gain feedback. Jesus understood this truth. He said that the world will know we are Christians by our love. That means love and service for one another (inside the circle) as well as for others outside the faith (outside the circle). If you look at Jesus's interaction with the apostles in the Upper Room in John 13:34–35, you will see the supreme measurement of discipleship—love for one another. But it doesn't stop there.

Later, when he prays in the garden as he heads to the cross, he describes aspects of a community that make it healthy and purposeful. Read John 17:6–26, where Jesus prays for his followers and for all future disciples. His prayer contains requests for his immediate followers (inside the circle) and for others who will one day follow him (outside the circle). Both kinds of requests are present.

WHAT IS HAPPENING *INSIDE* THE CIRCLE?

There are internal factors that require feedback and evaluation. These inner factors include, but are not limited to, the following areas.

Quality relationships
Processing conflict
Knowing spiritual gifts
Meeting group members' needs
Understanding biblical truth
Self-awareness and self-examination
Active listening
Healthy communication patterns
Leadership effectiveness
Apprentice development

By paying attention to these factors, the quality of group life can be enhanced. You want a healthy group environment and a culture within the group that fosters authentic community.

WHAT KIND OF IMPACT IS TAKING PLACE *OUTSIDE* THE CIRCLE?

It is necessary to measure a group by what is happening externally, with questions like:

How are we serving others?

Are we reaching people for Christ?

What have we done to add new members?

Are we preparing to launch another group?

These questions are important and must be addressed. An internal focus by itself falls short of the biblical wisdom for community. It is true that much of the Bible is focused on the internal working of a biblical community. And equally important, a healthy community is both a goal and the means to effective outreach and service. (Who wants to multiply the influence of an ineffective or dysfunctional group? What kind of impact does a group have if members lack character and aren't growing and the group is not becoming a Christlike community?) Nevertheless, external impact can also be an indicator of group health.

You can make copies of the table on pages 146–47, discuss additional areas for evaluation, and then allow each member to fill it out. Collect the responses and then, with some refreshments to foster a conversational tone versus a tone of hard critique, discuss the results and comments as a group. This will be a great exercise.

The key is to focus on healthy next steps and ways to improve. Make sure to celebrate what is working and commit to continuing the progress you have made in those areas.

RECEIVING FEEDBACK ABOUT YOUR LEADERSHIP

Group members need to provide direct feedback to you, the leader. This may be intimidating to them, but encourage them by insisting that it's vital to you. This feedback helps you lead them well! Use the following questions to prompt feedback. (It is okay to make a copy of this list and pass it out to members.)

Leadership Feedback Questions

1. What experiences with the leader outside the regular meeting times have been especially valuable to you?
2. What aspects of the leader's life do you most need (want) to observe so you can see a godly example?
3. What steps could your leader take, beyond leading the regular group meetings, to help you grow? (Be specific.)
4. Comment on the leader in the following areas:

- Availability outside of group times
- Approachability and concern
- Accountability and being firm, if necessary
- Sensitivity and compassion

5. Is there any other feedback you would like to give the leader?
6. Are there issues that are unresolved or require attention?
7. What affirmation can you give the leader—what aspect of the whole small group experience has been especially meaningful to you?
8. How will you pray for the leader?

HOW OFTEN SHOULD WE HOLD A FEEDBACK SESSION?

About every six months (perhaps three to four months if you meet weekly), the group should devote an extended amount of time, about thirty to forty-five minutes, to evaluating its progress. On the next pages, you will find some tools to help with that kind of meeting.

The key is to provide a climate of safety in which you discuss progress, name reality, give grace, and make changes *together* to improve personal growth, authentic community, and group effectiveness.

WHAT TO DO WITH THE RESULTS

Once everyone has filled out the Group Feedback and Evaluation table and you've had a group discussion, here are some ways to process the results.

1. Make sure everyone is clear on what needs to change and what can be celebrated.
2. Prioritize the next steps or changes, focusing on smaller items that can have a big impact. For example, in the area of logistics, maybe the group wants to change the time or day of meeting. Not a big deal but might help with lots of issues like attendance, childcare schedules, and work commitments.
3. Ask each member (or teams of members) to tackle a given issue. Don't try to tackle them all yourself. Assign proposed changes or improvements to others. Ask them to clearly identify the issue and to come back next meeting with a proposal for improvement. The group can engage the proposal and, after some discussion, decide what works best and how to make the change.

GROUP FEEDBACK AND EVALUATION

Inside the Circle			
	What's Working — Why?	What's Not Working — Why?	Changes or Next Steps
Quality Relationships			
Meeting Members' Needs			
Processing Conflict			
Healthy Communication			
Using our Gifts			
Self-Awareness			
Active Listening			
Knowing Biblical Truth			
Effective Leadership			
Shared Leadership			
Staying on Mission			
Logistics			
Ground Rules			
Prayer and Sharing			

Outside the Circle			
	What's Working — Why	What's Not Working — Why?	Changes or Next Steps
Serving Others			
Building Relationships			
Inviting New People			
Meeting Seekers			
Launching a New Leader or New Group			
Discovering Needs in the Local Community			

Results from Group Discussion

4. Affirm the process. Remind members how healthy this is for the group.
5. Set a date or time frame for doing this again (in six months, for example) so that it's a regular and normal part of your community.
6. Consider having a "group check-in" every four to six meetings. This is a five- to ten-minute discussion at the end of a meeting to simply identify any sticking points, any areas for clarification and growth, any needed midcourse corrections in vision or mission, or any other modifications that might improve overall group effectiveness. Doing this between your extended feedback sessions will make this session more focused and less dramatic.

SHARING RESULTS WITH YOUR CHURCH LEADERS

Asking others for feedback takes character and courage. I highly recommend it. Sadly, few people do this. Asking staff members (or others who support you as a leader) to look at your completed feedback forms will show that you want to grow. It will give the staff and others the information they need to provide you with focused training, resources, and information to help you lead well.

Your supporters and supervisors might already have a form or a process for giving you their feedback. If not, sharing your group's feedback with them will generate a good discussion and prompt them to be more intentional about giving you leadership feedback.

You can also give the questions on page 150 to the group or to your ministry leadership as a way of generating specific feedback.

WHAT IF THE FEEDBACK IS NEGATIVE?

Sometimes we get news we don't want to hear. An X-ray shows a spot; an annual review at work reveals that our boss is dissatisfied with our performance; a close friend or dating partner pulls away or wants to end the relationship.

"Negative" results may be exactly what we need to hear to grow spiritually and in our leadership, but it sure feels awful at the moment. I remember my first review at the bank where I worked after college. I sat in a chair, the office door closed, and my supervisor explained everything I had not done to build the business. It didn't matter that he had provided no clear goals for me to pursue. He had assumed that our training department (from which

I was the top graduate, making this worse) had told me exactly what to do in my new role. But it had not.

The reality was that he did not like what I was doing. It hurt, especially after twelve months of strong feedback and praise. It was emotionally awkward (though I held in the pain and anger) and professionally embarrassing. But one thing it did do. It set a benchmark and a context for a robust conversation about what was working and what was not. It redefined our relationship, clarified my work objectives, and provided me with an opportunity to grow in character and skills.

What did I do that allowed me to move from a defensive posture to a proactive one, from "That's not fair! You don't understand! Why didn't you tell me you wanted me to work in region X and on project Y?" to "Can we discuss what is expected in my role, how you want me to achieve those objectives, and what kind of relationship we need to build so I am fulfilling your expectations and the goals of the bank?"

1. *Clarify reality.* First make sure you have heard the feedback clearly. Our defensive posture and desire for self-justification will often keep us from listening to the truth (even though some of it may not be accurate from our perspective).

2. *Take time to think it through.* I took a day or so to mull over the review and then scheduled another meeting with my boss. I described my view of reality without being defensive, and it helped him understand my working style and strategy. Group members will appreciate that you took time to read through their feedback or think through verbal comments. It shows that you care and are willing to do some self-evaluation.

3. *Tell others what you plan to do with the information.* I acknowledged what I had heard and said I would set a time to work with my boss on a new strategy. In groups, let members know that you want to make changes based on their feedback. You took it to heart, thought it through, and have adjusted some things for the future.

4. *Ask for help.* I told my boss what I needed and expected from him. I needed clarity, some resources, and some mentoring from him in areas I was not exposed to in the training process. In the same way, tell the whole group or specific members what you need from them. In many cases, they will eagerly help and take responsibility for their part in making the group succeed.

REFLECTION

- How do I react to evaluation?

  Do I get defensive? Why?

  Do I become apprehensive? What is my fear?

  Do I see it as an opportunity for growth?

- What help do I need in order to process any negative feedback I might receive?

  Do I need to find a mentor?

  Do I need assistance from other group leaders?

  Do I need the help of a pastor?

Remember, feedback is your friend! You need it, the group needs it, and the ministry deserves it.

ADDITIONAL RESOURCES

Henry Cloud, Bill Donahue, and John Townsend, *ReGroup* (Zondervan, 2007). This DVD and training guide help a group become effective and include group check-ins so that groups can evaluate and measure growth. Includes teaching, dramas, and creative ideas.

Bill Donahue and Steve Gladen, *Building Biblical Community* (LifeWay, 2011). A group resource with DVD to help groups see what it looks like when a small group achieves success by becoming a celebrating group, a learning community, a loving community, and a serving community.

Bill Donahue and Russ Robinson, *Building a Life-Changing Small Group Ministry* (Zondervan, 2012). Uses seven strategic areas of focus for evaluating group life across the church, but also talks about group health and quality.

Patrick Lencioni, *The Five Dysfunctions of a Team* (Jossey-Bass, 2002). This leadership fable also includes the principles for becoming an effective team, many of which apply to group life and church teams as well.

Chapter 7

CARING FOR MEMBERS

Once you begin having meetings, developing relationships, engaging in the community-building process, and experiencing growth, you will be positioned to care for and support members. This section is focused on intentional encouragement and responsive care.

Your role is to become an encourager and caregiver, creating a caring environment in the group so you don't have to carry that burden alone. Here you will find tips for responding to care needs that are beyond the group's ability to handle.

The most rewarding ministry in small group life is caring for people as you help them move toward full devotion to Christ. Your group will become a safe and loving place for people as they face life's inevitable struggles and challenges. Group members will remember these defining moments for many years.

ENCOURAGING GROUP MEMBERS

Encouragement takes place when your love meets a member's fear.

Everyone has fears, disappointments, or confusion about life. Encouragement is showing others that we truly love them in the midst of their pain. Proverbs 18:21 says that the tongue has the power of death and life. Encouraging words bring life; shaming or harsh words bring death. Your job is to bring words of life to people who are feeling the sting of death emotionally. Listen to the instructions of Paul in Ephesians 4:29: "Do not let any unwholesome talk come out of your mouths, but only what is helpful for building others up according to their needs, that it may benefit those who listen."

Encouragement builds community.

Tips for Becoming an Encourager

1. *Be slow to speak* (Prov. 12:18; 13:3; James 1:19). A great way to encourage members is to listen to their stories with attentiveness and caring. Do not try to fix things quickly or offer glib answers to their problems or issues. Simply listen.

2. *Exercise sensitivity.* The Bible reminds us that our speech should be seasoned with salt. Our words should be filled with grace (Eph. 4:29) and should mimic those of Jesus, who came in grace and truth (John 1:14).

3. *Show kindness when you speak.* Words of gentleness are soothing and tender. Truth doesn't always have to be delivered from a rifle barrel. Truth spoken gently is more readily heard and more easily obeyed.

Pitfalls to Avoid When Giving Encouragement

1. *Defensiveness.* As you try to encourage others, some people might push back, saying, "You don't understand my situation!" Don't try to justify yourself. Simply listen to what they are saying and try to clarify what is being said.

2. *Sarcasm and criticism.* Sometimes people use humor to lighten the load or bring relief. As a leader, you might even use it to relieve tension and bring encouragement in the form of laughter. But sometimes humor gets out of hand and becomes biting sarcasm or hurtful criticism. Remember that people are easily wounded with words (Prov. 15:4).

3. *Correction.* Don't tell others that their feelings are wrong or inaccurate or say to them, "You shouldn't feel that way!" The point is, they *do* feel that way, and you need to listen carefully to determine why they have the feelings they are experiencing.

4. *Advice giving.* Avoid giving answers before having really investigated the questions (Prov. 18:13). Advice giving can be patronizing and can shut down communication. Quick advice often ignores the real problem.

Real encouragement requires active listening. It means fully engaging with another person and participating in his or her pain and frustration. As you listen carefully, you will be able to bring words of encouragement, comfort, and hope to people in your group. The Bible is full of exhortations and commands to build up and encourage one another with words. Skim through Proverbs 15–18 and notice how much wisdom is provided about the mouth, words, and the tongue. Reflect upon how you might incorporate some of these truths into your group's lifestyle.

REFLECTION

Encouragement Exercise

In chapter 5, there were many activities and ideas you can use to help your group members build relationships and encourage one another. Here is another.

Ask members to complete the following sentence for one designated member.

"(Name), I am so glad you are in this group, because . . ."

At various meetings, you can do this for different people, until your group has gone through all of its members. You could do this for everyone at a group retreat or extended gathering, but it is unlikely that you would do this for everyone at a regular group meeting.

As you complete the sentence, consider the person's character qualities, the person's actions, the person's contribution to the group, the person's gifts or talents, or simply the reason why you enjoy his or her presence in the group. The key is honesty and providing encouragement, not hype or merely general affirmation.

PROVIDING CARE TO MEMBERS

Giving care is part of the role of being a shepherd. God expects us to give the kind of care that he himself would give to his flock. This is clear from Ezekiel 34:1–16, in which God rebukes the shepherds of Israel for not giving appropriate care to the flock. As you study the passage, you see that God desires shepherds to

- feed the flock;
- lead them to rest;
- seek the lost;
- bring back the scattered;
- bind up the broken;
- strengthen the sick.

Being a shepherd is a huge responsibility. That is why it's important to share the care ministry with other members and particularly apprentice leaders. If you have too many people to care for, you will eventually burn out. How much care do you provide and how often? There are three levels of *fundamental* caregiving: personal care, mutual care, and backup care. Each is discussed in the next section. Crisis or *emergency* caregiving is covered in this chapter's next main section, titled "Handling a Crisis."

Levels of Fundamental Care

Personal care

Personal care is the direct support that a group leader is expected to provide for group members. Sometimes people belong to more than one group. Such care includes prayer support, phone calls, emails, encouragement, visits during times of illness, and finding resources to help meet needs.

You shouldn't have to provide such care to *every* member; the goal is to share this duty. There will be times when you might be the first (or only) nonfamily member or friend who can meet the care needs of a group member.

REFLECTION

Personal Care Considerations

1. Am I the best person to provide care to this member?
2. How can I provide care without creating a dependency on me as the only or primary caregiver?
3. In what way can I model caregiving for other group members so they can emulate some of what I do?
4. What specific caregiving approach is most comfortable to me, and where do I need to grow in my skills or delegate to others?

- Personal visit
- Email
- Letter
- Phone call
- Visiting with a partner (apprentice leader or another group member)
- Inviting the person to my home
- Meeting the person at church

Mutual care

Mutual care is the kind of care that group members give to one another. It is not possible (or expected) for a small group leader to provide all the care for all the members of the group. It is the goal of a small group to provide mutual, interactive care for one another. This kind of care includes taking meals to families with new babies, visiting people in the hospital, praying, and assisting with other needs. Such care enables us to fulfill the commandment in Galatians 6:2, which says, "Carry each other's burdens, and in this way you will fulfill the law of Christ."

REFLECTION

Mutual Care

1. Who in the group is most likely to share their care needs with me?
2. Try assigning care roles, such as in the list below, from time to time: think of each member of the group and jot down how they might best provide care to others.

Praying
Providing meals
Listening
Providing financial or other resources
Visiting
Creating a prayer chain or website to update needs

Backup care

Your first line of defense, backup care, is provided by your ministry leader or staff support. In some cases, this is a coach or some other volunteer who is responsible to care for and support group members. If your coach is unavailable, contact a pastor or other church leader or a ministry leader. Together you can work out a care strategy for the particular need you are seeking to meet. In some cases, a pastoral counselor or professional will be needed to meet the need and provide guidance.

Larger churches may have a care ministry designated to provide support in times of crisis or when a group is overwhelmed by the scope of the need (the death of a close family member, for example). You should make it your responsibility to discover now—not later—who is the best person or team to contact about intense or emergency care needs.

Caring for People in Pain: Guidelines

Pain (emotional, physical, spiritual) presents us with an opportunity for growth

C. S. Lewis wrote, "God whispers to us in our pleasures, speaks in our conscience, but shouts in our pains. It is his megaphone to rouse a deaf world."

"Pain is the gift nobody wants," said Philip Yancey.

These are true sayings, but we don't feel better when we hear them in the midst of our suffering. Pain has a way of capturing our attention, often to the point where we can think of little else.

And yes, pain provides an opportunity for each of us to become better or bitter—it depends on our response. But leaders cannot take responsibility for making others feel better. And we cannot preach victory messages to people in pain.

The opportunity for growth is as real as the experience of pain, grief, and loss. As we mature in Christ, we are able to thank God—as Christians have through the centuries—for lessons only pain can teach us. There is a certain bond to Christ, the suffering servant, that we discover when we share in his sufferings on earth. If we are able to receive this gift, then we are able to say more fully, "I am crucified with Christ." Not easy … but true.

Hurting people value your presence over your words or skills

"I feel helpless around people in pain. Helpless and guilty. I stand beside them, watching facial features contort and listening to their sighs and moans, deeply aware of the huge gulf between us. I cannot penetrate their suffering, I can only watch. Whatever I attempt to say seems weak and stiff, as if I'd memorized the lines for a school play" (Philip Yancey, *Where Is God When It Hurts*, p. 15).

Here is the truth: There is little you can do or say—no magic wand to wave—to relieve the pain of others. But you can walk with them, as Jesus walks with each of us in our pain.

Our first response may be to do something. But what most people want first is our love, acceptance, and presence. To sit with them at the funeral, wait with them in the hospital, cry with them at the bedside of a cancer-stricken child. These are the acts of a leader when members suffer.

Shared pain is often the gateway to community and group growth

When our pain is brought into community, we find deeper love, grace, hope, and healing. It seems the more people present with us, carrying our burdens with us (Gal. 6:2), the more we experience mercy and hope.

Groups that suffer together mature together.

Is there someone in the group who needs a pain partner right now?

REFLECTION

Providing Care

What is your greatest concern as you think of your responsibility to provide care?

Which of the following resources or actions would you consider using to express care or concern to people when they need help?

- The support of elders or staff members
- Sharing the need (with permission) with other groups or leaders
- Sharing the need (with permission) with other care ministries in the church

HANDLING A CRISIS

From time to time in a small group, an emergency or crisis may occur. Members will look to you, as the leader, in times of crisis.

In Cases of Impending Physical Danger

Contact the police immediately. Such crises would include:

- Life-threatening situations
- Severe accidents or emergencies
- An attempted suicide or threatened suicide
- Present threats of violence by a person to himself or herself or to others
- Dangerous, illegal behavior by group members (sexual assault, selling drugs, and so on)

Though it is very unlikely that you will ever experience any or most of these in the context of a group meeting (or even with members of your group in other contexts), please be aware of the possibility and know that you should contact the authorities immediately.

Note: Check with your pastoral staff on all of this. Each state has different laws regarding your responsibility to report illegal behavior and regarding whom it should be reported to.

Other Serious Situations

If you have a serious situation that requires help and guidance (for example, child abuse or neglect, spousal abuse, and so on), contact your coach and church immediately for aid in discerning the severity of the crisis and for assistance in reporting the incident to the proper authorities.

Remember, in most situations, your first point of contact should be your ministry leadership. If there is any threat of violence or danger, call the authorities immediately.

SUPPORTING VERSUS COUNSELING

As a small group leader, you are expected to provide support and encouragement to members of your group. However, you are not trained to be a professional counselor, so you should not assume such a role. Instead, your responsibility is to provide opportunities for your members to receive the care they need. Situations that may require professional help:

- Serious marriage problems
- History of past abuse
- Addictions
- Severe personality disorders
- Mental disorders or dysfunctions

If you encounter anything that resembles the examples above, contact your coach to see what steps to take. Together you can make a plan for encouraging a group member to get counseling or some other type of help. Never contact a church leader directly and give a member's name. In such cases, it is imperative that you do not violate a person's right to confidentiality.

Just because you think someone is in need of counseling does not mean they will be willing to get counseling. Work with your coach and with ministry leaders at the church to determine how to approach an individual with the suggestion of counseling or other help.

What if attempts toward help and care are not readily received or are even rejected?

There are people who will reject your desire to provide care. If you have not already experienced this, you will. It is a hard thing to fathom. You see a need, try to act and express love, and the person rejects you, appearing to have a hard heart. Here are some suggestions.

The Bible says we should seek peace with all people (James 3:17; Heb. 12:14), so don't push your help on the person.

Challenge the person lovingly. Ask him or her to let you help. Remind the person that the body of Christ works best when everyone helps one another.

Ask the person, "How can we help?" because maybe you misunderstood the need or offered the wrong kind of help.

Ask why the person rejects legitimate help that is obviously needed. Is it fear, pride, shame, or something else that is in the way?

Ask if you can at least pray for the person. That's always a start. If the person rejects even that, say that you will still pray for him or her in your private prayer time.

We are not psychologists, and neither can we peer into a person's soul—only God can do that. Do what you can, offer what you can, don't be afraid to gently challenge or ask why help is being rejected, and then leave the person in God's hands.

ADDITIONAL RESOURCES

David Augsburger, *Caring Enough to Confront* (Herald Press, 2009). A great balanced approach to dealing with conflict in a group.

William Backus, *Telling Each Other the Truth* (Bethany House, 2006). As the title implies, this resource offers guidelines for speaking the truth to each other in love, especially when the truth is hard to communicate.

Larry Crabb, *Shattered Dreams* (Waterbrook, 2010). Acknowledges that pain and suffering are real and must be embraced in community.

Lawrence Crabb Jr. and Dan B. Allender, *Encouragement* (Zondervan, 1990). A classic book on how to build into the heart and lives of others.

John Ortberg, *Everybody's Normal Till You Get to Know Them* (Zondervan, 2003). Creatively describes what relationships look like, including the challenging aspects of working with people.

Philip Yancey, *Disappointment with God* (Zondervan, 1997). Deals with the perceived silence of God, and what to do when he does not meet our expectations or answer our prayers.

Philip Yancey, *Where Is God When It Hurts?* (Zondervan, 2002). Describes our relationship with God as we process personal pain and loss.

Chapter 8

IMPACTING YOUR WORLD

Behind the vision "No one stands alone" are several desires for group life in the church:

- *No one grows alone.* It takes a community of Christ followers to help each person grow in faith.
- *No one suffers alone.* A caring, loving community provides resources and support in times of crisis and need.
- *No one serves alone.* There is great power in numbers, and a group can accomplish so much more than can any one member when there is a project to complete.
- *No one seeks alone.* When people join together to investigate the claims of Christ, they impact each other with their stories and lives.

Since we have already addressed the first two desires listed above, this chapter is devoted to the last two desires. Learn to support one another as you serve the needs in the world around you. Discover how to create a place where new people—especially non-Christians—can find a place in community. In each of these ways, your group can have lasting, profound impact in the lives of others.

As you serve people and invite people into community, your group will grow. If you have been investing in the development of an apprentice or two, you will have the capacity to care for new members as the group adds people.

GOD WANTS TO GROW HIS COMMUNITY

By inviting others to join your group and training your apprentice, you are creating an environment for multiplication. To help you in this process, there are resources for inviting others and for giving life to a new group.

Since the beginning of time, it has been God's desire to create a people who would have fellowship with him for all eternity. Though he enjoyed perfect fellowship as a tri-unity (Father, Son, Holy Spirit), God wanted to expand that community to all who put their faith in him. From Genesis to Revelation, we see God's heart in reaching people and including them in this new community.

The promise of a Messiah (Gen. 3:15).

The promise to Noah (Gen. 9:8 – 17).

The promise to Abraham to make him a great nation (Gen. 12:1 – 5).

God's promise to make the Israelites his people (Ex. 6:7).

God's promise to David of an eternal kingdom and a place for God's people to dwell (2 Sam. 7:1 – 17).

God desires to be known among all nations of the earth (Ps. 67).

The invitation for all to come and be part of God's community (Isa. 55:1 – 3).

The promise of a Messiah who would become known throughout the earth (Mic. 5:2 – 5).

God will be known among all the nations of the earth (Zeph. 3:8 – 10, 20).

The invitation for all to come and receive Christ (Matt. 11:28 – 30).

The command to make disciples of all nations (Matt. 28:18 – 20).

The promise that all who believe will become part of a new community through the Holy Spirit (1 Cor. 12:13).

The power of the Holy Spirit will enable all believers to witness for Christ (Acts 1:8).

The world will not hear the gospel unless we take it to them (Rom. 10:14 – 15).

As you can see, God has been inviting people into his community for centuries. This is evident in a personal way in the life of Jesus. Jesus built relationships with people like Nicodemus, the woman at the well, the woman caught in adultery, and the twelve disciples—and his invitation to join him in relationship continues today. Andrew invited Peter, Barnabas introduced Saul to a fledgling church, and Paul reached out to Timothy and others as he built churches and expanded the ministry.

Part of discipleship is reaching out to people who are not involved in biblical community. This includes seekers, fringe Christians, and committed believers who are seeking fellowship.

INVITING OTHERS TO EXPERIENCE GROUP LIFE

Maybe you have been asking, "How do I connect new people to our group?" Here are some steps to think through and a chart that will help you brainstorm the names of people who could potentially be added to your group.

Step 1: Before You Begin Inviting New Members

1. Involve everyone in the process. Everyone in your group should consider how to invite someone to the group.
2. Teach the group to provide a "seat at the table" for someone, and have the group discuss what that means.
3. Regularly pray for God to bring people into the group.
4. Develop a list of potential members.

Step 2: How to Invite New Members

1. Allow potential members to meet other members of the group before they ever attend a group meeting.
2. Explain the vision of your group to the potential member.
3. Ask potential members to think about and pray about joining the group.
4. Develop relationships between the potential member and other members of the group before the potential member attends a group meeting.
5. Allow potential members to attend a few social gatherings or meetings before joining.

REFLECTION

Finding Potential Members

Using the following categories, jot down names of people with whom you already have relationships or with whom you could build relationships.

Faith. People who are disconnected from your church:

continued on next page

Family. People in your immediate or extended family:

Friends. Your friends and the friends of other members of your group:

Firm. People with whom you work or do business:

Step 3: After New Members Attend the Group
1. Affirm the new member and the one who brought him or her.
2. Have everyone briefly retell some stories about their journey into your group.
3. Celebrate what is happening in your group.
4. Reaffirm or revise (with the newcomer's input) group values and covenant or ground rules.
5. Allow the group to assimilate new members and to grow together for a season before inviting additional people. No one wants to stifle growth; this is just a broad guideline. A revolving door of people in and out of a small group of eight to twelve can be a bit crazy. Add people, then help them get connected and settled into the group.

Note: This is a general process for inviting people to groups. Consult your ministry leaders to determine whether all components of this process apply to your particular kind of group. (For example, seeker or explorer groups might use a different process for inviting non-Christians into a group, and a task-oriented group may have specific guidelines that relate to accomplishing the task.)

CONVERSATIONS WITH PROSPECTIVE MEMBERS

Getting to know someone in a short time requires some focus and skill. Even people who make a living meeting other people will tell you that it takes time to make a connection and build trust. In a small group situation, success often hinges on a leader's ability to help a potential member find common ground with other members so that he or she will feel at home in a new group.

Here are some areas in which to ask questions in order to find common ground and build relationships. Questions that foster friendship based on common ground can be grouped into four broad areas:

1. Background
2. Job and family
3. Interests and hobbies
4. Spiritual appetite

Here are some examples. As you meet with potential members one on one or with other group members, don't feel pressured to use all of these questions. Pick the ones that you feel comfortable with or that best suit your needs. You might even want to write your own or rephrase these into your own words.

Background

1. How did you happen to come to this church and/or group?
2. Where did you go to church before coming here?
3. Are you from the area? Where did you go to school?
4. What was your church background growing up?

Job and Family

1. What do you do for a living? What did you do before your current job?
2. Do you enjoy your current position? If not, what's your dream job?
3. What's your schedule like? How busy are you with your job?
4. How long have you been married? Do you have any children? If so, how many?
5. How would you describe your relationship with your spouse? How do you stay connected on a daily basis?
6. What has been the most challenging thing about being married (or single)?

7. What has been the most rewarding thing about being married (or single)?
8. Tell us about your extended family. Do you see your parents much? How many brothers and sisters do you have?

Interests and Hobbies
1. What do you like to do with your free time? Do you have any hobbies?
2. What do you like to do when you go out?
3. What do you do to relax?
4. Is there any new sport, activity, or hobby you would like to learn?

Spiritual Appetite
1. Have you ever been in a small group before, here or at another church? What did you enjoy about it?
2. Why are you looking to join a small group?
3. How are things going spiritually? How's your walk with God?
4. What do you think you can bring to the lives of others in the small group?
5. What are your expectations for the group? What do you want to see accomplished?
6. Where do you hope to be spiritually when our time together as a group is finished?

Please note the design and progression of these questions. Direct inquiries into spiritual specifics or a person's walk with God can be threatening. Consequently, ask the simple, nonthreatening questions first. This will loosen them up, and it will probably loosen *you* up too!

As the conversation flows, mentally note what you are feeling about it as well as what the person is saying. His or her body posture, tone of voice, facial expressions, or glances at a spouse all create reactions within you that can help you see if there is a connection or if the conversation is awkward for the person. Don't make judgments too quickly and neglect really hearing what is said. Seek to understand and to find a connection that can become the first step toward a group relationship.

INVITING SPIRITUAL SEEKERS TO GROUPS

Some groups are not prepared to receive people with spiritual questions. At particular stages, either the nature of the material being studied or the personalities and experiences of group members can prohibit groups from effectively welcoming seekers. If your group desires to open up to seekers, you may want to work with your ministry leadership to help prepare your group for this process. For example, you would want to be sensitive in the following areas when inviting seekers to a group meeting or to a social event.

- Focus on the needs of the seeker, not on your personal agenda.
- If you discuss a Bible passage, use a version of Scripture that is seeker friendly (*The Message*, Today's New International Version, and *The Journey* are good examples).
- Stay away from religious lingo or religious clichés such as "Hallelujah," "Amen, brother," "Lamb of God," or "I'm just trusting in the Blood." Such terminology is biblical but unfamiliar to seekers, and it might scare them away, because they will feel like they don't fit in the group.
- Focus on relevancy. Don't get too caught up in theological arguments or distinctions. Stick with the basic truths of Scripture.
- Allow seekers to make comments that might appear strong or opinionated. Don't argue with them. Thank them for their input, and help the group respect a seeker's questions or point of view. Listen more than you talk!
- Keep prayers simple. Use normal, conversational language when speaking to God. Help a seeker see that prayer is simply talking with God, and not some religious jargon.
- Don't shy away from hard issues or places where even some believers have doubts. Be honest. Be truthful. Don't be afraid of speaking biblical truth—just be sure to allow dialogue and to explain unfamiliar Bible terms or concepts.

These are just a few tips to give you an idea of sensitivities you need to have toward seekers. Some seekers might fit better in a seeker-targeted small group because of the nature of their questions. Many will feel welcome in a typical group. Before inviting seekers to any group, devise a strategy that will best serve the seeker and the group.

LAUNCHING A NEW GROUP FROM YOUR GROUP

1. Cast a vision for a new group from the onset of your group, especially if an apprentice leader is present.
2. Include this goal in your ground rules or covenant.

3. Prepare the apprentice for group leadership.
4. Help the group understand that one purpose of the group is to give life to new groups.
5. Help the group catch a vision for reaching those who are not yet in Christian community.
6. Several months before launching a new group, begin the process of breaking into subgroups for some part of every meeting. This means that the apprentice leader and the leader each lead a smaller group for part of the meeting. This often occurs in two rooms of the same house or apartment. Breaking into subgroups allows members to begin to feel the process of separation from other group members or from the apprentice. The goal is not to divide the group but to give some structure to the new group that is forming. It is likely that you will grow to fourteen to sixteen members before considering this process.
7. The leader and apprentice should each be seeking new apprentices in preparation for the launch. Make sure these new apprentices each work with one of the subgroups.
8. Begin meeting as two groups for most of the meeting time.
9. At the time of launch, celebrate the beginning of a new group.

Launch Day

Launch day is a time for celebration. As the new group begins to finally separate from the existing group, it's time to gather together and celebrate new life. Here are some ways to celebrate the joys and experience the loss of launching a new group from the existing core.

1. Have a time of celebration for what God is doing.
2. Hold a time of prayer as you commission and bless the two groups.
3. Recognize and affirm the leadership in each group.
4. Allow members to express their feelings of celebration and sadness. (Remember, you can still meet as one large group as often as you like. This is a process, not an abrupt tearing apart of two communities.)
5. Plan a set time when the two groups will come together, if this is not part of the regular strategy (probably in four to six weeks).
6. Have a time of communion together and share the victories and blessings of each group.
7. Spend time praying about the future of both groups and about what God might do to help each grow spiritually and numerically.

8. Have each member write a letter to the rest of the group expressing their feelings of thankfulness and respect.
9. Take pictures or videos of the groups as you prepare to launch.
10. Set a schedule for a few planned social events together in the future so that the group reunites on a regular basis.

Launching Strategies

The chart on page 170 presents four ways of launching groups.

REFLECTION

Launching a Group

What launching strategies might work best for our group? Can we design our own?

What might the timetable for us to give life to another group look like?

What needs to be done to find or develop an apprentice who can lead a new group (or take over this group if I and others set out to launch a new group)?

Launching New Groups

Original Group   *New Group*

Leader Launches New Group

Apprentice becomes leader
Finds new apprentice
Same members

→

Original leader leaves
Finds new apprentice
Finds new members

Apprentice Launches New Group

Leader stays
Finds new apprentice
Same members

→

Apprentice leaves,
becomes new leader
Finds new apprentice
Finds new members

Core Group Launches New Group

Leader stays
Finds new apprentice
Some members stay
Some new members
added

→

Apprentice leaves,
becomes new leader
Finds new apprentice
Some members follow
Finds additional new
members

"Turbo" — All Members Launch New Groups

All members are
apprentices who start a new
group individually or in pairs
Leader starts new group

→

Apprentice becomes
new leader
Finds new apprentice
Finds new members

Apprentice becomes
new leader
Finds new apprentice
Finds new members

Apprentice becomes
new leader
Finds new apprentice
Finds new members

Wisely Navigating the Launch

To reduce the fear or concerns associated with launching a new group:

1. Talk about the goal from the beginning. Talk about the desire to multiply your influence with optimism and vision. If the idea of launching a group is thrown at members at the last minute, there will be anger and resentment.
2. Help the apprentice leader(s) to succeed by giving him or her leadership opportunities.
3. Honor "core units" of two or three who should remain in relationship.
4. Allow time for this transition.
5. Have a party when the launch occurs.
6. Periodically or regularly get the two groups together.
7. Encourage grief work. People will experience sadness at the "loss" of group members and should be encouraged to talk about this. Don't simply move ahead as if such sadness didn't exist. Relationships matter, and people sense they might lose some aspect of their relationships now that certain members have left the original group and joined the new group. Remind them that though they will likely see these people at church and at other gatherings, their absence from the group each month is something everyone feels.
8. Prepare to strategically add new members to the group.
9. Be pastoral and encouraging during the process, not driven by some agenda.
10. Meet with individual group members after a group has birthed, in order to process the birth on a one-to-one basis.

A new launch is like a miniature church-plant because the sending community is launching a new community, and this can be exciting as well as challenging. If you keep this analogy in mind, it will help you maintain a sense of vision and celebration for the new thing, while understanding that there may be a sense of loss or sadness about changing the nature and scope of the relationships built in the existing group.

Launch Follow-Up

Once the new group has launched out of the existing group, both should spend a meeting or two processing what has taken place. This will help groups to officially separate, to celebrate, and to express feelings about the process. Also, you should begin to pray about adding new members to the new groups. The existing group should take a few meetings to reorient as a core group, and then begin the process of inviting people into this new community, smaller now and able to receive some new folks.

Remember, the existing group is now a new group, because it is not the same as it was before. Leaders must give particular attention to group members during this time, as they may be experiencing feelings of sadness, frustration, or loss.

Other Considerations

Groups launch a new group at various rates. The key is not the number of meetings before launch as much as it is the preparation of the apprentice leader. Groups are ready to launch when apprentices are ready to lead and have identified new members and potential apprentice leaders. A group can multiply at anywhere from nine to thirty-six months, but it will vary by ministry and by group, depending on how often the group meets, the readiness of the apprentice, and the nature of the ministry.

From time to time some launches are not successful. It is difficult for the new group to get started. In such cases, work closely with your ministry leaders and determine what the best solution is. Things in life don't always work out perfectly, and the same is true of small groups. Spend time in prayer asking God to give you wisdom for the situation.

When adding seekers to existing groups, be thoughtful. The best way to destroy a group—and damage seekers—is to bring them into it when the group is not prepared to receive them. This could also seriously damage a seeker's opinion of Jesus or the church. If you are passionate about working with seekers (and feel gifted in this area), then you might think about developing an apprentice who can take over your group as you branch out to lead a seeker-targeted group filled with people asking questions about God and the church.

There are always some people who have difficulty developing relationships. Perhaps they don't know anyone because they just moved into the area, or perhaps they've had difficulty with social skills or are very introverted. This doesn't mean they can't participate in small groups. Talk with your ministry leaders to find ways to incorporate such people into your group. If you know of someone who has difficulty connecting to a group, contact your ministry leaders and discuss a strategy for helping him or her get involved.

Effective Communication of the Gospel

Reaching out to new people is exciting and will often involve conversations with many who do not yet know Christ. Here are some helpful suggestions for evangelistic conversations and relationships. Though evangelism is not the goal of a relationship ("The only reason why I care about you is because I think you might become a follower of Christ"), engaging in spiritual conversations with people is a call of the gospel and the privilege of every believer.

Evangelism should be natural

The Scripture is clear that you don't need the gift of evangelism to be an effective communicator of the faith. Paul encouraged Timothy and the members of the church in Ephesus to "do the work of an evangelist" (2 Tim. 4:5). Once you understand your style of evangelism, you will be more effective at doing that work.

Your style may vary from that of someone else, but the responsibility to share our faith rests with each of us. Some people use a confrontational style, some an intellectual style, some a relational style. Whatever your style, remember to be natural and to be yourself.

Evangelism is relational

Begin by developing friendships with people who are not in a relationship with God. Most of us need to build relationships with people prior to sharing the gospel with them. Develop authentic relationships with friends and acquaintances.

Evangelism is verbal

Romans 10:14 asks the question, "How, then, can they call on the one they have not believed in? And how can they believe in the one of whom they have not heard? And how can they hear without someone preaching to them?" Ultimately, we must share Christ in a conversation in which we communicate the facts of the Christian gospel through our personal testimony, the reading of Scripture, or some other method.

Evangelism is team-oriented

There is personal evangelism, but there is strength, help, and a diversity of interaction when a group is involved in leading someone to faith. I remember a friend who trusted Christ while in our group. His comment later was, "I watched how all of you lived your lives, not just what you said. That was very powerful."

Effective evangelism often includes inviting people to events and gatherings that will clarify the gospel or demonstrate the love of Christ. Churches must mobilize all of the resources at their disposal to create the environment for such events and gatherings. You need not share your faith alone. Use the resources of your church to help people hear the gospel in a variety of forms and presentations.

To see an example of a conversation with a seeker, we focus on Jesus Christ's interaction with the Samaritan woman at the well. As you read through this scene in John 4, certain principles become obvious. Though Christ shared the gospel in different ways with different people, this is a basic example of a loving yet direct conversation with someone who has spiritual interests.

REFLECTION

Who in the group needs help or skill training in order to become more effective in evangelistic relationships and conversations?

Who do I or the members of the group know who is gifted or experienced in this area, so that we can invite him or her to come to a group meeting and help us all grow in our awareness, skills, and compassion for people outside the body of Christ?

An example of a Christ-centered spiritual conversation: John 4

Every evangelistic conversation and process is different. This is not a model of what to do; it's an example. There are some things to learn from it. You should also look at other encounters Jesus had with people like the rich young ruler (Luke 18), Nicodemus (John 3), the Pharisees (John 8:12–30), and others. There was no formula or three common steps. This doesn't mean that some methods we use today aren't helpful; it simply means that we start with the person, not just a process.

Here are some insights from John 4.

1. vv.1–8: Jesus is culturally relevant.

   a. *Speak their language.* In that culture, water was an important topic of discussion.

   b. *Discover a felt need, a point of mutual interest.* This woman was lonely and ashamed of her life. And she was looking for water at a time of day when because of the heat, no one went to the well.

2. vv. 9–10: Jesus piques her curiosity.

   a. *Ask good questions; listen.* Be interested in the other person and in what he or she is thinking and saying.

   b. *Don't always be the one talking.* In a sense, Jesus asked, "What do you think living water is?" Seekers are turned off by people who have all the answers; listen to them and give them an opportunity to talk about their concerns.

3. vv. 11–12: Jesus creates interest by offering solutions to her deepest needs.

   The issue is the person of Jesus Christ. People are focused on their needs (in this case, water). Jesus finds common ground in the area of need (water) and builds a bridge. Bridge building is key to the development of any trusting relationship.

4. vv.13–15: Jesus offers to meet her need.

   Jesus turns the discussion toward himself (living water and life) as the solution to a spiritual problem (the spiritual dryness and thirst of a soul disconnected from him). She is still focused on her felt need. She is also living a life in fear, shame, and sin. She's had many relationships, probably mostly out of fear. In the ancient world, a woman living alone was likely to live in extreme poverty and isolation.

5. vv. 16–24: Jesus's conversation leads to a discussion of the true nature of God and a personal encounter with the true Messiah and the life he offers.

   We lead someone to Jesus. We talk about life with the living God. The Holy Spirit does the work of illumination (opening the person's eyes to truth), and transformation of the heart takes place. The person recognizes the Messiah and follows.

6. vv. 25–26: Jesus wants people to become followers, not religious people.

   a. *Be a true worshiper of God.* Being a true worshiper is living in a relationship with God, not following a set of rules.

   b. *Follow Jesus.* When Jesus reveals himself as the true Messiah and Savior, the woman follows him and leads others to this amazing person (4:39ff.).

Important verses for evangelism

God desires a personal relationship with you

"Jesus declared, 'I am the bread of life. He who comes to me will never go hungry, and he who believes in me will never be thirsty'" (John 6:35 NIV).

"Whoever believes in me, as the Scripture has said, streams of living water will flow from within him" (John 7:38 NIV).

"The thief comes only to steal and kill and destroy; I have come that they may have life, and have it to the full" (John 10:10).

Sin keeps us from a personal relationship with God

"All have sinned and fall short of the glory of God" (Rom. 3:23).

"The wages of sin is death, but the gift of God is eternal life in Christ Jesus our Lord" (Rom. 6:23).

You must receive Jesus Christ and place your faith in him

"To all who received him, to those who believed in his name, he gave the right to become children of God" (John 1:12 NIV).

"If you confess with your mouth, 'Jesus is Lord,' and believe in your heart that God raised him from the dead, you will be saved" (Rom. 10:9 NIV).

"It is by grace you have been saved, through faith — and this is not from yourselves, it is the gift of God — not by works, so that no one can boast" (Eph. 2:8–9).

If you place your faith in Christ, your eternal life with him begins now and is secure

"This is the testimony: God has given us eternal life, and this life is in his Son. He who has the Son has life; he who does not have the Son of God does not have life. I write these things to you who believe in the name of the Son of God so that you may know that you have eternal life" (1 John 5:11–13 NIV).

REFLECTION

What are the opportunities for our group to reach out to non-Christians through relationships, acts of service, and strategic gatherings?

Relationships. Who can we be praying for?

Acts of service. Who can we serve?

Strategic gatherings. What can we design, or what is happening in our church, that we can leverage for connecting with non-Christians?

SERVING OTHERS OUTSIDE THE GROUP

Reaching out beyond the group involves inviting people into community, sharing the gospel with people, and serving people in need. Every group member who seeks to follow Christ is called to serve others in obedience to the gospel and by using their gifts.

There are three primary ways to serve others: serve one another *inside* the group (we covered this in the sections on caring for one another), serving *individually outside* the group, and serving others *as a group*.

Serving Individually, Supported by the Group

A group can be catalytic in empowering every member for service. It is difficult for many groups to serve together as a unit. Work schedules, family commitments, illnesses, and other conflicts may prevent 100 percent attendance at serving opportunities.

Individual service (or service with a couple other members from the group) is easier to coordinate and celebrate. In order to help people in your group move toward a serving lifestyle, here are a few strategic considerations.

1. *Use the Bible to teach people about serving.* Key verses include:

   "Do you see those who are skilled in their work? They will serve before kings; they will not serve before officials of low rank" (Prov. 22:29).

   "Even the Son of Man did not come to be served, but to serve, and to give his life as a ransom for many" (Mark 10:45).

   "Each of you should use whatever gift you have received to serve others, as faithful stewards of God's grace in its various forms" (1 Peter 4:10).

   "We have different gifts, according to the grace given to each of us. If your gift is prophesying, then prophesy in accordance with your faith; if it is serving, then serve; if it is teaching, then teach; if it is to encourage, then give encouragement; if it is giving, then give generously; if it is to lead, do it diligently; if it is to show mercy, do it cheerfully" (Rom. 12:6–8).

   "Those who have served well gain an excellent standing and great assurance in their faith in Christ Jesus" (1 Tim. 3:13).

   "Whoever serves me must follow me; and where I am, my servant also will be. My Father will honor the one who serves me" (John 12:26).

   "The greatest among you should be like the youngest, and the one who rules like the one who serves" (Luke 22:26).

   "You, my brothers and sisters, were called to be free. But do not use your freedom to indulge the sinful nature; rather, serve one another humbly in love" (Gal. 5:13).

   "Be shepherds of God's flock that is under your care, watching over them—not because you must, but because you are willing, as God wants you to be; not pursuing dishonest gain, but eager to serve" (1 Peter 5:2).

2. *Model a servant lifestyle.* Jesus came to serve and not be served (Mark 10:45). And he gave up prestige and position and even refused to exercise some of his power in order to serve others as God in the flesh (Phil. 2:5 – 11). So asking, "How may I help you?" is the posture of every leader toward group members and toward others.

3. *Help members discover their gifts, wisdom, and experience in order to serve others.* Encourage members to try a variety of ministry opportunities through church, through other groups, or simply as needs arise through personal interactions.

4. *Share serving experiences.* When you gather as a group, share what individual members have been doing, as a means of motivating one another to serve.

5. *Brainstorm new ideas.* Study your local community and describe the opportunities that exist to help single mothers, the poor, the homeless, families with sons and daughters in the military or in harm's way, and so on. Look for people in need of home repairs, businesses to serve, social agencies to partner with, and the like.

Serving as a Group

Here are ways to serve together that you can discuss and explore as a group.

1. *Serve together monthly.* Help at a local soup kitchen, serve at a food pantry, tutor some kids, help at a local school, and so on.

2. *Put a date or two on the calendar.* If you cannot create a regular rhythm, identify some dates that the entire group can set aside. Make sure everyone knows that this is a commitment. If you are serving with a group or agency, you must show up! Don't let them plan for ten of you to come for five hours, and they have five of you come for three hours. Honor your commitments! *Note:* This is the biggest complaint people have about those who volunteer to serve — volunteers checking out at the last minute because of a conflict (often not a serious one, usually just inconvenient).

3. *Decide to serve as a group but rotate the members.* The group takes responsibility for a regular serving opportunity but promises that a set number (three or four, for example) will always be there to serve. All members of the group are trained and able to serve, but it will not be the same people going to serve each time. In this way, a group can own a meaningful serving project or effort, always fulfill the

commitment, and involve every member of the group over a period of time.

The key is a lifestyle of service. Sometimes this will be structured; sometimes it will simply be a personal or group response to an immediate need. If your group is on mission with its values and commitments, service will soon become a way of life, not simply an occasional event.

ADDITIONAL RESOURCES

Scott Boren, *Missional Small Groups* (Baker). How to make a difference in the world through your group. Helps a group truly have impact in the culture and look outside its own needs.

John Burke, *No Perfect People Allowed* (Zondervan, 2005). Looks at the five barriers emerging generations face as they view church culture. This is a great tool to help your group understand people in their twenties and thirties and why they think Christianity is out of touch with reality.

Bill Hybels and Mark Mittelberg, *Becoming a Contagious Christian* (book and training materials) (Zondervan, 1996, 2007). This approach helps each person identify their personal evangelistic style (storytelling, confrontation, relational, etc.) so that evangelism is more natural and less programmed.

Will Miller and Glenn Sparks, *Refrigerator Rights* (Berkeley, 2002; Willow Creek, 2008). Highlights our need for close connections with neighbors and friends to ensure our health, reduce our stress, and aid the well-being of society.

Rebecca Pippert, *Out of the Saltshaker* (InterVarsity). This is another great book about how to be salt and light in the world so as to impact people with the gospel.

KINDS OF SMALL GROUPS

	Age/Stage Based	Need Based	Task/Mission Based	Interest Based
Examples of Groups in This Category	Couples', families', men's, singles', women's	Recovery groups, grief support, postabortion, etc.	Food pantry, greeters, vocal teams, mission teams, etc.	Sports, computers, seekers, bikers, etc.
Curriculum	Chosen by leader/ group	Specified by staff	Chosen by leader/ group	Chosen by leader/group
Typical Lifespan of Group	2–3 years; many continue longer	Usually 9 weeks; can be repeated	As long as task is needed	1–2 years; many continue longer
Meeting Frequency	2–3 times per month	Usually weekly	Usually weekly	2 times per month
Open Group	Yes, for entire lifespan of group	Groups close after third week	Yes, but depends on nature of task	Yes, for entire lifespan of group
Seekers Welcome	Yes	Yes	Yes (except staff teams, elders, etc.)	Yes
Typical Focus	Community, study, prayer	Healing, comfort, connection	Service, community, prayer	Connection, community, study
Role of Leader	Connect people to community	Provide a safe place in a crisis	Complete the task and care for members	Connect people to community
Multiplication	Usually every 24 months; if apprentice is ready	Not usually — group lasts only 9 weeks	As often as task may demand and apprentice is ready	As appropriate; if apprentice is ready
Apprentice	Yes	Yes	Yes	Yes

RELATIONSHIP-BUILDING EXERCISES

*H*e is able" *celebration.* Ask your group members to bring to your next meeting a tangible item that represents how God has proven himself able in their own lives recently. Ask them to be prepared to explain how God has been able and how that item represents God's ability to act and bless.

- It should be a physical item that members can hold up and talk about.
- Members should talk about their own experience (not someone else's).
- Ask members to relate a recent experience they have had.

At the meeting, let each person relate his or her story. You may wish to close this time by all singing the song "He Is Able."
Variation: "God answers prayer" celebration

"Remember when." In the Scriptures, we often see God's people recounting the past experiences they have had or remembering God's deeds. This can be done in a variety of ways.

- Remember how you first heard about Christ.
- Give your testimony.
- Remember times when God answered prayer.
- Remember when God brought you through a difficult situation.
- If your group has been together for a while, remember things you have been through together and what they meant to you.
- Retell the story of first coming to your church, and explain what the church has meant to you.

This exercise builds a sense of history with your group if you've been together for a while. Recounting God's character or your experiences can be a prelude to a time of worship.

Two truths, one lie. Give everyone in the group a sheet of paper and a pen or marker. Have everyone write down two true things about themselves and one lie. These can be in any order. (Have them write big enough so the paper can be held up for everyone to see.) Then have someone hold up his or her paper and read the three items aloud. Everyone must guess which item is a lie. The person then explains why each item is a truth or a lie. Have every member take a turn.

Questions in a hat. Before your meeting, fill a hat (or bowl) with opener questions on individual pieces of paper (one question on each piece of paper). Have at least as many questions as there are people in the group. Vary the depth of the questions so they are appropriate for your group. Add the following special things on separate pieces of paper and put them in the hat.

"Pass to the right"
"Pass to the left"
"Boomerang (back to you)"

At the beginning, state that everyone always has the right to pass on any question (to put people at ease so they don't feel put on the spot). Someone, let's say Mary, picks a question out of the hat. Mary can ask anyone in the room (but just one person) to answer that question. She asks John. After John answers the question, he picks a question and asks anyone in the room *except* Mary, and so on.

If you pull one of the special pieces of paper out of the hat, save it and use it when someone asks you a question. If you use a "Pass to the right," then the person on your right must answer the question. If you use a "Pass to the left," then the person on your left must answer the question. If you have a "Boomerang," then the person who asked you the question must answer it. (Of course, anyone can pass at any time if he or she wishes.)

"Who am I?" During the week before your meeting, collect one unknown fact about each person in the group, from that person. This should be something the group members will not mind being revealed. Type a list of these facts (including one for yourself). Make enough copies so that everyone has a list. (Since you know them all, just facilitate the exercise. If they guess yours, just tell them!)

At the meeting, hand out the lists. The objective is for group members to find out which fact matches which person. Each member may approach another member and ask about two items on the list. ("Are you the one who …" If not, then "Are you the one who …"). After two inquiries, the member must move on to someone else.

After a time limit (or as soon as someone gets them all), stop the game and read through the list, identifying everyone.

Draw a time line of your life. Give everyone a long sheet of paper and pens or markers. Have each group member draw a time line of his or her life, showing three to five major life events. The number of events can vary, depending on how much time you have during your meeting. Then let each member explain what he or she drew.

Draw a self-portrait. Give everyone a large sheet of paper and markers or crayons. Have each person draw a self-portrait. Collect all the self-portraits, hold them up one by one, and have group members guess who each represents. When someone matches a self-portrait with the artist, have the artist tell a little about himself or herself.

Introductions. When introductions are needed, instead of everyone introducing themselves, ask each person to let someone else in the group introduce him or her. If it's a couples' group, have the spouses introduce each other. This can be very affirming.

Videos. Videos can be used for times of worship, praise, or singing. Or use a video camera to film episodes of *A Day in the Life*, each featuring a different group member.

Subgroups. If your group is large enough, break it up into smaller groups, even pairs, for various activities. This is especially useful for times of prayer, sharing on a personal level, allowing relationships to deepen, and dealing with sensitive subjects.

Attributes of God. Ask, "What attribute of God has been especially meaningful to you lately?" (For example, "I really appreciate God's faithfulness to me because …")

Have each person in the group talk about this, and share your input as well. *Variation: Don't talk about it — go right to prayer and pray through it.*

Their names in a verse. Pick a topic ahead of time and choose verses on that topic — one verse for each member of the group and one for yourself. During prayer time, have each person read their assigned verse with their name in it and pray through that verse.

For example, the topic is "God's love for us." Verses chosen could be Psalm 13:5–6, John 15:9, Romans 5:5, and so on. One of the group members reads aloud Psalm 13:5–6: "I, Sandy, trust in your unfailing love; my heart rejoices in your salvation. I will sing to you, Lord, for you have been good to me."

Serve each other. Look for opportunities to serve each other outside of group time. This will go a long way in developing your relationships with each other. How about

- painting a room in someone's house;

- doing a large cleaning project;
- bringing meals when help is needed.

Serving others together. Look for opportunities to serve as a group, providing help, support, or encouragement to someone else. Here are a few things you can do.

- Help a needy family or person(s).
- Serve at church during a special event (for example, provide childcare for Easter service).
- Look into an international ministries opportunity.

Celebrate. Search for things to celebrate: groups starting, birthing, growing; personal accomplishments; the end of a season of your group; a successful experience. Be creative in the way you celebrate. Enjoy being together!

"It's a wonderful life." In advance, secretly ask three close friends (may include the spouse) of each group member to write out what the world would be like if that person had never been born. Before reading these aloud, cue up the scene from the classic movie when George Bailey tells the angel Clarence it would be better if he had never lived, and the angel has an idea to show him how the world would have suffered.

After viewing the video, read one of the three letters aloud for each person. Allow time for the group to comment. (Note: this may take two meetings. Keep it to five minutes per member.)

Gauges. Give each person a white sheet of cardboard that you have prepared in advance by writing the following categories on the left margin.

Emotional *(Am I in touch with my feelings?)*
Relational *(What is the quality of my family relationships and friendships?)*
Physical and Recreational *(Am I healthy? Am I having any fun?)*
Ministry Fulfillment *(What is my joy level in ministry?)*
Spiritual *(How honest and growing is my relationship with God these days?)*

Make available to the group members colored pieces of tape or markers of different colors. Have each person take time to analyze each dimension of his or her life and stick a piece of tape or draw a wide band of color next to each gauge. Colors have the following meanings.

Green: I am flourishing in this area.
Gray: I am doing okay; nothing too great, nothing too bad.
Yellow: I have growing concerns for this area. Caution!

Red: I am in trouble in this area. It requires serious attention and correction.

Then have each person hold up his or her card and explain what the gauges indicate.

Hot seat. Call each group member, one at a time, to sit on a seat in the room, facing everyone. Then have the person on the hot seat choose a question from a pile and answer it. Invite members of the group to pose follow-up questions or discuss the person's responses for the next three to four minutes.

Sample questions for this exercise might include:

"What is your favorite book of the Bible and why?"
"Lately I am becoming more ..."
"The feeling that best describes where I'm at right now is ..."
"If there were one person in the world who I could spend a day with, that would be ..."

Member appreciation night. Give each member of the group a piece of paper with his or her name at the top. Have them draw lines on the paper to create enough boxes for all of the people in the room. Then have them write this sentence underneath their name at the top of the sheet: "I appreciate this person because he or she ..." Tell everyone to pass these sheets around the room so that each member can complete the sentence by filling in one box. After all the sheets are completed, have members return them to their owners. Then allow each member to share what impresses him or her most about the affirmation he or she received from others in the group. (This should take approximately thirty to forty-five minutes.)

Life story. Over a period of several weeks, have each member of your small group spend fifteen minutes telling his or her life story. Then allow fifteen minutes for discussion and interaction. The point of the exercise is to find out exactly where people have come from. Often it's hard to appreciate people until we understand their past and some of the significant events in their lives.

Group Communion service. The purpose of this is to share in the Bread and the Cup as a small group. This can be an incredibly meaningful experience.

Each person, one at a time, personally serves another group member. (You can assign whom they will serve in advance or simply move around the circle.) As you serve one another, make appropriate comments about the love of Christ, specifically for the individual being served. When you are done, the group closes in a time of prayer and/or worship.

Three key material possessions. Set up the scene as follows: Explain to the group that they have just discovered a major fire in their home. Assuming they have gotten their family safely out, what three *material* possessions would they take with them from their burning home? Have members explain why they would take the items they chose. Then generate a discussion to discover the value behind each of these possessions and why we hold certain possessions so dear.

Group photo. The purpose of this exercise is to have each member take a "picture" of the group. In other words, have each person make a drawing or use a word picture to describe what the group looks like. For example, the group could be described as any of the following:

- A hospital (a place where wounds are healed)
- A gas station (a place to be refueled spiritually)
- A fortress (a safe place where struggles can be shared)
- A debating team (a place where we can wrestle with truth or differences of opinion)
- A mountaintop (a place to gain perspective and be encouraged)
- A valley (a place of discouragement and trial)
- A carnival (a place for fun, enthusiasm, and excitement)

These are just some examples, but have members either draw or describe the kind of group environment they need or see.

Fill in the blank. Ask various members of the group the following fill-in-the-blank questions.

1. "Something I will most likely take for granted tomorrow is ..."
2. "Last year at this time, I never would have thought that God would ..."
3. "The person I am most thankful for this year is ... because he or she ..."
4. "One specific attribute of God which I most appreciate is that he is ..."
5. "God used the following people to enrich my life this past year: ..."
6. "I want to thank the Lord for giving me the gift of ..., so I can use it to serve him and the church."
7. "Considering the standard of living of most of the world's population, I am rich because I have these material blessings: ..."
8. "If I could stand up and shout anything to the rest of the body of Christ tonight, I would tell them that ..."
9. "My God is ..."

THE ANALYTIC METHOD OF BIBLE STUDY

Here is a more detailed use of the "engage and examine" approach we discussed in chapter 2. It's a more analytical and informational approach, used to gain insight into the original meaning of a passage.

1. OBSERVATION (WHAT DOES THE TEXT SAY?)

Use several translations. Read the entire passage through several times. Try using several different translations (NIV, NASB, TNIV, NKJV, *The Living Bible*, *The Message*, and so on) for a fresh look at the passage each time you read it. This will help you identify key words and develop insights into the text.

Context. Answer the following in writing.

1. Who is writing or speaking and to whom? What is their relationship?
2. What is discussed? What is happening?
3. Where does the event or communication take place?
4. When does this take place relative to other significant events?
5. Why does the speaker say what he does? (What problems were the recipients facing?)
6. How does this passage fit into the context? (For example, what comes before and after?) How is God using this text to speak to me?

Structure. Examine the structure of the passage and make note of any significant connecting words that help you understand the author's argument (for example, *therefore, but, and,* and so on). Try to paraphrase the passage, using your own words. Are there any key words that help you understand the author's emphasis?

Word study. List all key words of the passage and use a Bible dictionary (such as *Vine's Expository Dictionary* or *Richard's Expository Dictionary of Bible Words*) or a good study Bible (such as the *NIV Study Bible*) to understand their meaning.

Questions. Write answers to the following as you read the passage.

1. What are the commands to obey?
2. What are the promises I can trust God to keep?

3. What do I learn about God? About Jesus? About the Holy Spirit? About my fellow believers?
4. Are there any repeated words, ideas, themes?
5. Are there any comparisons or contrasts (for example, "flesh" vs. "Spirit" in Romans 8)?
6. Are there any lists (like the fruit of the Spirit in Gal. 5:22–23)?
7. Are there any cause-and-effect relationships (such as in Rom. 10:14–18)?

2. INTERPRETATION (WHAT MESSAGE DOES THE TEXT CONVEY?)

Truths. List specific points of truth from your observation of the text. Bombard the passage with questions that relate to its meaning. Proceed verse by verse, recording your understanding as you ask yourself questions like, What does this mean? Why is it important to understand this? How did this relate to the original audience? What is the opposite of this truth? When should this be applied? How should it be applied in my life?

Look up cross-references to help you interpret the passage. Also, trust the Holy Spirit as your teacher. Pray, asking him to reveal God's truth to you.

Commentaries. Consult any commentaries you can and write down insights they have that you might have missed. Call wise teachers or leaders in the church to gain their perspective. Ask people in your small group to look at the passage with you.

Themes. Write down in a sentence the main idea or point you think the author is trying to get across. You may want to write down two or three main principles you discovered that develop the theme.

3. APPLICATION (WILL I ALLOW SCRIPTURE TO TRANSFORM MY LIFE?)

"All Scripture is God-breathed and is useful for teaching, rebuking, correcting and training in righteousness."

—2 Timothy 3:16

Teaching. Ask, How will this truth change my life, my church, my family, my work?

Reproof. Ask, Where do I fall short? Why do I fall short?

Correction. Ask, What will I do about it? What will I correct? How will others help me do this?

Training in righteousness. Ask, What practices, relationships, and experiences will I pursue so that I might train myself to be like Christ?

Building a Life-Changing Small Group Ministry

A Strategic Guide for Leading Group Life in Your Church

Bill Donahue and Russ Robinson

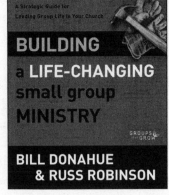

In *Building a Life-Changing Small Group Ministry*, part of the Groups That Grow series of small group resources, authors Bill Donahue and Russ Robinson provide guidance for the strategic decisions that must be made to establish, develop, and grow a thriving small group ministry in the local church.

They answer questions like: • Which approach or model for small group ministry is best for my church? • Who has responsibility for the ministry and how are they supported? • How do I organize the groups and coach the leaders? • Where do I find leaders and what kind of training do they need? • How do I guide people toward community life? What are the pathways and events that move people to become part of a small group? • What kinds of groups should we offer? • How do you multiply groups and launch new groups? • How do we define success in this ministry?

As you work through the questions in each chapter, you'll develop a coherent, strategic plan for building and leading the small group ministry at your church. And whether you are establishing a new ministry or transitioning from older models of small group ministry that are no longer effective today, you'll benefit from the time-tested wisdom of the authors. This workbook can be used as a stand-alone resource or it can be used with the five-session training videos taught by the authors available on the *Equipping Life-Changing Small Groups DVD* (sold separately).

Available in stores and online!

Coaching Life-Changing Small Group Leaders

Bill Donahue and Greg Bowman

Small groups transform churches—and lives. Small group leaders often feel the weight of shepherding their small group members. But who shepherds the shepherd?

Small group coaches fill a unique role by providing support and guidance for group leaders. When you're called to coach a small group leader in your church, your mind may be filled with questions: Am I godly enough? What do I have to offer? How do I begin? Although the challenge seems immense, Bill Donahue and Greg Bowman break down the work of coaching small group leaders into achievable steps.

This expanded and updated edition offers field-tested and biblically supported advice on such topics as modeling a surrendered life to those you coach, gaining the tools and wisdom you need for coaching, and helping leaders grow spiritually. This workbook can be used as a stand-alone resource to train coaches, or it can be used with the training videos taught by the authors, available on the *Equipping Life-Changing Small Groups DVD* (sold separately). For those who want to coach with excellence and truly help small group leaders thrive, this go-to guide offers practical answers and inspiring examples. You'll find both challenge and promise in these pages as you learn to carry forth your God-given calling with confidence

Available in stores and online!

Groups That Grow

Equipping Life-Changing Leaders

Focused Training for Group Leaders, Coaches, and Pastors

Bill Donahue with Russ Robinson and Greg Bowman

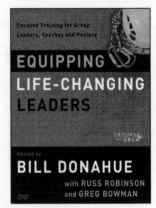

The *Equipping Life-Changing Small Group Leaders DVD* contains video training curriculum that works side-by-side with the Groups That Grow series of small group resources to effectively train small group leaders and the coaches who shepherd them, ultimately building a stronger, more vibrant small group network in your church. This' DVD contains a total of 17 sessions of training encompassing three hours of teaching.

Along with practical teaching and time-tested lessons shared by small group ministry experts Bill Donahue, Greg Bowman, and Russ Robinson, training sessions include interviews with small group leaders and role play reenactments of real-life challenges that small group leaders often face.

Three different curriculums are included on the DVD, each matching a different book in the Groups That Grow series of resources, including:

- Leading Life-Changing Small Groups (8 Sessions)
- Coaching Life-Changing Small Group Leaders (4 Sessions)
- Building a Life-Changing Small Group Ministry (5 Sessions)

Facilitator's guides (in PDF format) are also included on the DVD to assist those leading the training and teaching sessions, providing suggestions on how to best use the video content with the material in the books.

For those who want to effectively equip small group leaders and coaches with excellence and truly witness life change in their small group ministry, this video-based training offers practical answers and inspiring examples.

Available in stores and online!

.com